What people are saying about

THE SECRET BATTLE OF IDEAS ABOUT GOD

"We're in a battle for our hearts and minds. *The Secret Battle of Ideas about God* not only diagnoses the disease—it writes the prescription to cure it. As CEO of Summit Ministries, Dr. Jeff Myers has been in the trenches and foxholes of spiritual warfare. He doesn't offer a sugar-coated salvation free from pain, problems, and pressure. Instead, he shows how a Christian worldview defeats the bad ideas that spread like viruses and multiply our misery. *The Secret Battle of Ideas about God* is hopeful, but it's also deeply honest—and that's what gives it such value. We're all in the fight: *The Secret Battle of Ideas about God* is a combat manual for winning."

Mike Huckabee, former governor
of Arkansas, regular contributor to
Fox News, author, and speaker

"Jeff Myers's brilliant and compelling *The Secret Battle of Ideas about God* is like a handbook on how to navigate life on earth. Ideas are what will help us or kill us. The good ideas, which happen to be true, help us live even when life is difficult; and the bad ideas, which are lies, kill us from the inside. I'm thrilled my friend has written this important primer on one of the most important subjects there is: what we believe and how that affects everything else. May God use this book!"

Eric Metaxas, author of *Bonhoeffer* and host of
the nationally syndicated Eric Metaxas Show

"What good is it to complain about our ailments if we won't seek the remedy? *The Secret Battle of Ideas about God* takes us inside the hidden battle that rages for our hearts and souls so we can see what attracts us to corrupt ideas and find the healing that comes from discovering the truth. Jeff and Summit have given us another worldview classic."

Del Tackett, DM, host of The Truth Project

"Dr. Jeff Myers has devoted his life to studying worldview issues. He teaches students how to understand the differing perspectives that fill the culture around us. More importantly, he equips us to defend and communicate the Christian worldview in a way that articulates the truth in love. This book is sure to be a helpful resource."

Jim Daly, president of Focus on the Family

"There is no better authority on matters of worldview than Jeff Myers. He's eminently qualified as a professor and the president of Summit Ministries, and he's uniquely gifted as a man who has experienced the consequence of bad ideas. In *The Secret Battle of Ideas about God*, Dr. Myers shows readers how five deadly worldviews threaten to rob each of us of the love, healing, purpose, and peace found in Jesus. If you're struggling to see God's hand in your life, or if you've ever felt alone or abandoned as a Christ follower, this book is a God-send. *The Secret Battle of Ideas about God* will help you think clearly about your Christian walk and equip you to share the power of the Christian worldview with others."

J. Warner Wallace, bestselling author of
Cold-Case Christianity and *God's Crime Scene*

"Jeff Myers has led faithfully and thoughtfully for years in the arena of worldview and apologetics. This book is an accessible primer, targeted to equip a new generation to think through big issues. We need a resurgence of thought and action on applying the gospel to the questions around us. This book can help."

Russell Moore, PhD, president of the
Ethics & Religious Liberty Commission
of the Southern Baptist Convention

"Ideas matter. In fact, they matter a lot. Unfortunately, too many people—including Christians—are unaware of them and how they work. That's why this book is so important. In *The Secret Battle of Ideas about God*, Jeff Myers unlocks how ideas are claiming our allegiance, both personally and culturally. It's a captivating read, and so, so critical for all of us."

John Stonestreet, president of the Colson
Center for Christian Worldview

"Jeff Myers has written some powerful and timely books. I would venture to say that *The Secret Battle of Ideas about God* is his best yet. He deconstructs five 'fatal' worldviews of today by exposing their logical inconsistencies, but more importantly, he shows that they fail to fulfill the deepest needs of the human heart. With insight and vulnerability, Myers shows both the uniqueness and the power of the Christian worldview. This book will be a game changer for those willing to read it with an open heart."

Sean McDowell, PhD, professor at
Biola University, speaker, and bestselling
author of *A New Kind of Apologist*

"*The Secret Battle of Ideas about God* is a gripping page-turner that reveals how bad ideas are infecting Christians today, undermining their influence in society, and squelching their boldness for Christ. The author, Dr. Jeff Myers, is president of Summit Ministries, the undisputed gold standard for teaching a biblical worldview. This is Summit at its best—fascinating insights delivered in a deeply personal way that inspires confidence to live differently, starting now."

Jim Garlow, PhD, senior pastor of
Skyline Church, La Mesa, California

"With vivid stories and a vulnerable heart, Dr. Jeff Myers identifies the pervasive, misguided logic of our day and how to answer opposing worldviews that render us spiritually anemic. *The Secret Battle of Ideas about God* is exactly what any good doctor would prescribe for a culture that is riddled with confusion and noise about God and who he is."

Jack Hibbs, pastor of Calvary
Chapel Chino Hills, CA

"Parents: if you want your kids to choose the truth and follow Christ, this is a must-read. Your children's worldviews affect everything in their lives, and you play a vital role in forming it. In *The Secret Battle of Ideas about God*, Dr. Myers offers an unforgettable way to spot and defeat bad ideas that attack us like viruses. Using easy-to-understand language and vibrant illustrations, he shows you how to disciple your children toward a worldview based on Jesus so they can stay strong and not waver in a culture waiting to infect them with lies. Read this practical, important book!"

Kathy Koch, PhD, founder and
president of Celebrate Kids, Inc.

"Dr. Jeff Myers and Summit Ministries have done it again! *The Secret Battle of Ideas about God* is a clear and succinct introduction to the devastating effects of bad idea viruses. Every church leader, member, and Christian school teacher needs the inoculation of biblical truth found in this intriguing work to stop the infectious indoctrination of impure ideas about God and biblical truth."

Wesley Scott, EdD, PhD, executive
director of the Southern Baptist
Association of Christian Schools

"There's a critically important battle of worldviews going on in our culture, yet many people don't even realize they're the casualties of bad ideas. Jeff concisely yet powerfully arms readers with an understanding of the battle lines, shows why only Jesus can win the war, and offers corresponding practical insights for daily living. His willingness to share his own struggles makes this an especially compelling read for anyone who wants to better understand the difference a person's worldview makes."

Natasha Crain, author of *Keeping Your Kids on God's Side* and *Talking with Your Kids about God*

"Ideas comprise the seeds that shape individuals and societies. Most followers of Christ would agree that the garden of our culture is being overtaken by deadly, destructive weeds. But why? How? Where do these vicious vines come from? What can we do in response? Within these impactful pages, Jeff Myers takes us under the soil of both our lives and culture to explore what he aptly refers to as *The Secret Battle of Ideas about God*. In ways that are both substantive and practical, he helps us understand how ideas shape our worldview and also how we can deliberately cultivate the right kind of thinking that will generate health in our individual lives and also in our culture."

Matt Heard, founder of THRIVE and author of *Life with a Capital L*

"*The Secret Battle of Ideas about God* shows how Jesus wins against the bad ideas that attack our nation like viruses. This is biblical worldview made very, very practical. A must-read to understand the call to truth and action."

Alveda C. King, evangelist and
guardian of the King Family Legacy

"Someone once said that if you embrace bad ideas, at some time in the future you will attend a banquet of consequences. That's true of worldviews too. In this helpful book, Jeff Myers unpacks the personal implications of the ideas we embrace about God. It's not just a survey of worldviews, but a personal, practical, 'what difference does it really make' worldview tour book. It will help you discover which ideas are toxic, and which ideas are life-giving and lead to freedom."

Don Sweeting, PhD, president of
Colorado Christian University

"My long-admired friend of many years, Jeff Myers, has profoundly impacted my life and the lives of those I love most in this world. *The Secret Battle of Ideas about God* displays his signature ability to draw deep lessons from life's stories and the metaphors that express truth all around us. *The Secret Battle of Ideas about God* reminds us that we're in a conflict that requires both choices and action—and that we truly can have clarity and live differently to the glory of God."

Peter W. Teague, EdD, president
of Lancaster Bible College

THE SECRET BATTLE OF IDEAS

ABOUT GOD

ANSWERS TO LIFE'S BIGGEST QUESTIONS

JEFF MYERS

SUMMIT

DAVID C COOK

transforming lives together

THE SECRET BATTLE OF IDEAS ABOUT GOD
Published by David C Cook
4050 Lee Vance Drive
Colorado Springs, CO 80918 U.S.A.

Integrity Music Limited, a Division of David C Cook
Eastbourne, East Sussex BN23 6NT, England

The graphic circle C logo is a registered trademark of David C Cook.

The website addresses recommended throughout this book are offered as a resource to you. These websites are not intended in any way to be or imply an endorsement on the part of David C Cook, nor do we vouch for their content.

LCCN 2017931378
Paperback ISBN 978-0-8307-7634-4
Hardcover ISBN 978-1-4347-0965-3
eISBN 978-0-7814-1412-8

© 2017 Summit Ministries

The Team: Tim Peterson, Ron Lee, Cara Iverson, Abby DeBenedittis, Susan Murdock
Cover Design: Jon Middel
Cover Photo: Getty Images

Printed in the United States of America
First Edition 2017

1 2 3 4 5 6 7 8 9 10

051018

For the battle is the L<small>ORD</small>'s.

1 Samuel 17:47

CONTENTS

FOREWORD   15

CHAPTER 1: INVISIBLE WARFARE   19
    The Hidden Forces That Shape Our Lives

CHAPTER 2: STOPPING BAD IDEAS   31
    Four Things to Do When You're on the Brink of the
    Apocalypse

CHAPTER 3: AM I LOVED?   45
    How Idea Viruses Make Us Feel Unappreciated,
    Unwanted, and Alone

CHAPTER 4: LOVE NEVER FAILS   59
    How Jesus Meets Our Hearts' Deepest Longings

CHAPTER 5: WHY DO I HURT?   73
    How Idea Viruses Fail Us in Our Suffering

CHAPTER 6: WE SHALL OVERCOME   85
    How Jesus Heals Our Hurts and Gives Us the Victory

CHAPTER 7: DOES MY LIFE HAVE MEANING?   99
    How Idea Viruses Strip Us of Direction and Leave Us
    Aimless

CHAPTER 8: HEARING THE CALL   111
    How Jesus Restores Meaning to Our Lives

CHAPTER 9: WHY CAN'T WE JUST GET ALONG?   127
    How Idea Viruses Destroy the Peace We Crave

CHAPTER 10: PEACE WINS   143
How Jesus Offers the Elusive Harmony We All Seek

CHAPTER 11: IS THERE ANY HOPE FOR THE WORLD?   157
How Idea Viruses Drive Us to Despair

CHAPTER 12: HOPE ENDURES   171
How Jesus Restores Hope in the Midst of Despair

CHAPTER 13: IS GOD EVEN RELEVANT?   185
How Jesus Conquers Idea Viruses Once and for All

ACKNOWLEDGMENTS   201
NOTES   205

FOREWORD

It's easy to see what people do, but harder to see what underlying ideas power their actions. Yet *what* we think and *how* we think matter. Whether or not we perceive it, at the core of ideas humans have about the world is a theological understanding of reality. This book helps peel back the layers so we can think theologically about the ideas that shape people's lives, thereby enabling we who follow Jesus to respond to people and circumstances in more Christlike ways.

Looking deeper than mere actions—examining underlying patterns of thinking and worldview—has been a hallmark of Barna Group's research for decades. In his book *Think Like Jesus*, my mentor George Barna defined a *biblical worldview* as "a means of experiencing, interpreting, and responding to reality in light of biblical perspective."[1] Following in George's pioneering steps, our team at Barna has studied the relevance and role of the biblical worldview in Americans' lives, and our tracking since 1995 shows continuity over the course of two decades—until recently. Data from the past five years suggest the 10 percent of US adults who have historically held a biblical worldview is on the decline; in 2015, just 6 percent of Americans qualified under George's definition.

We expect the trend to continue because, during the past half decade, cultural changes have shifted into overdrive. As Gabe Lyons and I explore in our book *Good Faith*, nominally Judeo-Christian (biblical) cultural moorings have given way to a new moral code—the morality of self-fulfillment, characterized by perspectives like the following:

THE NEW MORAL CODE[2]

*Please indicate whether you agree or disagree
with each of the following statements.*
% "completely" + "somewhat" agree

	% US Adults	% Practicing Christians
The best way to find yourself is by looking within yourself	91	76
People should not criticize someone else's life choices	89	76
To be fulfilled in life, you should pursue the things you desire most	86	72
The highest goal of life is to enjoy it as much as possible	84	66
People can believe whatever they want, as long as those beliefs don't affect society	79	61
Any kind of sexual expression between two consenting adults is acceptable	69	40

Source: Barna OmniPoll, August 2015, N=1,000.

As you can see, even practicing Christians accept these non-biblical worldview statements in astonishing numbers—and questions of morality are not the only place nonbiblical worldviews are creeping in. The Barna team, commissioned by Summit Ministries, conducted new research among practicing Christians to assess the encroaching influence of the ideas examined in this book (for details, visit www.secretbattlebook.com/research). Strong agreement with ideas unique to these five non-Christian worldviews is widespread among practicing Christians:

- 61 percent agree with ideas rooted in new spirituality.
- 54 percent resonate with postmodernist views.
- 38 percent are sympathetic to the teachings of Islam.
- 36 percent accept ideas associated with Marxism.
- 29 percent believe ideas based on secularism.

These churchgoers certainly are not "responding to reality in light of biblical perspective"—and that's a problem if our hope is to be a light for the world, pointing people loved by God to the way of Jesus. How can we point the way if we can't even stay on the path?

That's the first reason I'm so thrilled my friend Jeff Myers has written this book—because only good theology and clear thinking can cure bad theology and muddled thinking. In order to thrive as exiles in what I've come to call "digital Babylon," we need a shot in the arm like *The Secret Battle of Ideas about God* to inoculate us against the worldview viruses that suffuse the cultural air we breathe.

We also need understanding and wisdom to help others recover from infection. Jeff's thorough study of nonbiblical worldviews in *The Secret Battle of Ideas about God* will help you identify what people believe and why—but, just as importantly, his grace-filled guidance for how to engage people will help you respond to them with kindness and love.

And that's the second reason I'm honored to recommend this book: because if "I understood all of God's secret plans and possessed all knowledge … but didn't love others, I would be nothing" (1 Cor. 13:2 NLT). Jeff offers rich knowledge in *The Secret Battle of Ideas about God*, but he does so with humility and compassion, never arrogance or condescension.

As we look beyond mere actions into the world of ideas, I pray we will do the same.

David Kinnaman
President, Barna Group
Ventura, California
March 2017

CHAPTER 1

INVISIBLE WARFARE

The Hidden Forces That Shape Our Lives

Deanna Williamson has said she never heard the explosion. She just saw paper floating through the air outside, like a ticker-tape parade.

A stockbroker from California, Deanna was in Manhattan attending a training conference for employees of the investment firm Morgan Stanley. As attendees gathered in the south tower of the World Trade Center, in a conference room on the sixty-first floor, Deanna slipped out to get a cup of coffee. That's when green paper fluttering down outside a window caught her attention.

Soon Deanna and her coworkers saw desks falling from upper stories of the other high-rise and balls of fire erupting. Later they saw people plummeting to their deaths from the north tower.

This isn't happening.

Several minutes passed as the Morgan Stanley employees stared in disbelief. At last, security guards rushed down the hallway and broke the spell, directing the group to the nearest exit. They descended flight after flight of stairs. Deanna's anxiety grew when she started smelling smoke. *Is our building on fire too? Will we all die of suffocation before we reach the street?*

They were sixty floors from safety. With thousands of people being evacuated from the 110-story tower, progress was painfully slow. It was a New York pedestrian traffic jam on a relatively narrow stairwell. Shuffle. Wait. Repeat.

Deanna's thoughts turned to her husband, who just then was halfway around the world in Australia. She found herself longing for the family they hoped to have. And now it might never happen.

Suddenly the building lurched hard. It felt as though they were being shaken by a major earthquake, which Deanna had experienced in California. That's when she began talking to God.

God, I want to thank you …

The lights went out, emergency lights went on, and searing heat engulfed the stairwell.

… that this is happening to me and not to my family, my parents, my husband.

As she prayed, her attention was drawn to a woman sitting on the stairs, crying. "I'm a single mom. I'll never see my baby again."

"It's okay," Deanna said, taking the woman's hand and pulling her up. "Let's get out of here."

As they descended seemingly endless flights of stairs, word came that their building had been hit by a jet. Unknowingly, the workers fleeing for their lives had become frontline troops in a secret battle. A catastrophic idea had been released in the world, and now it was spreading, virus-like, claiming victims without remorse.

This was the end, Deanna sensed. Then she realized she had left her purse—along with her ID card—in the conference room. *When they find my body*, she realized, *the searchers won't know who I am.*

───────

Rick Rescorla, Morgan Stanley's head of security, *had* heard the first explosion that came from the north tower. He knew instinctively it was the opening salvo of a new kind of war. A decorated military hero, Rick had spent the past few years studying ideas that were multiplying while remaining largely hidden. In many regions of the world, there was growing resentment toward the United States, he sensed, but Americans for the most part were oblivious to the danger.

Having heard the blast from the adjacent tower, Rick knew he needed to act. He picked up the phone and called the Port Authority office in Midtown Manhattan. He was told to stay calm and keep people in their offices. It's safer in the building, the official said. Slamming down the receiver, Rick pulled out his cell phone and dialed his best friend, Dan Hill, a war veteran like himself.

"You watching TV?"

"Yes," Dan said, instantly connecting the dots. *Rick was at the World Trade Center.*

Exploding in colorful language, Rick rumbled, "They told me not to evacuate. They said it's just Building One. I told them I'm getting my people out of here."[1]

Rick jabbed the "End" button and grabbed two pieces of equipment. A photo taken that day shows Rick as a heavyset man holding a bullhorn in one hand and a walkie-talkie in the other, directing the evacuation of Morgan Stanley's World Trade Center employees.

The ideas that had shaped Rick's life came together that day. He became a hero, saving thousands of lives. The people he saved said he was singing the whole time. And in that seemingly random fact—that a hero acted quickly and with great foresight, while singing—we find a clue to how to win the battle that rages around us.

WE'RE IN A SECRET BATTLE

We live in a time of war. There are no soldiers in this battle. There are no landing craft, no bombers flying in formation, no artillery emplacements. Yet attacks occur every minute of every day.

The battle we're in is a battle of ideas. Ideas are thoughts and suggestions about what we ought to do. Our ideas largely determine our understanding of life's meaning and guide us in the way we live. Everyone forms ideas about questions such as the following:

- **Am I loved?** If I were to disappear, would anyone miss me?
- **Why do I hurt?** Bad things have happened to me. Can I overcome them and find joy?
- **Does my life have meaning?** Is it possible for me to find direction in life?
- **Why can't we just get along?** What will it take for us to stop fighting and find harmony?

- **Is there any hope for the world?** So many
  things seem to be going wrong. Are we doomed?

The set of ideas that we form in answer to these questions is called a worldview. A worldview monitors the ideas we are exposed to and isolates the ones that appear to be destructive. But it's possible to have a worldview that is porous, letting through some of the most damaging ideas. Or a worldview might be skewed in some way, welcoming ideas bent on doing us harm.

The battle of ideas never lets up, so how can we remain standing against such an onslaught? We need a healthy worldview that accurately identifies the ideas that come at us from every direction. We catch ideas from church, from culture, from family, and from friends. Billboards, speeches, songs, video clips, memes, pictures, Facebook posts, and lines from movie dialogue all present us with fragments of ideas that assemble themselves in our minds. If we are to live whole, satisfying lives, we need to do two things. First, we have to catch good ideas, and second, we have to avoid catching bad ones.

Unfortunately, bad ideas are easy to catch because they share a distinguishing characteristic with one of the deadliest things in the physical world.

BAD IDEAS ARE LIKE VIRUSES

The battles we face are more like germ warfare than like military warfare. That's because bad ideas are like viruses. A virus is genetic material coated by protein. Genetic material is common and ordinarily not harmful. Proteins are necessary for the body to do its work. Separately they're harmless. When combined, however, they can be deadly.

Bad ideas can multiply out of control, like the spread of a virus that becomes a pandemic. And even though idea viruses cause mass destruction, the battle we face is a secret battle because it's hard to accurately identify bad ideas until after they have struck.[2]

Idea viruses hover around us like secret agents waiting to infiltrate. Is there anything we can do to prevent them from sickening our souls and ruining our lives? I believe there is. That's what *The Secret Battle of Ideas about God* is about. We'll learn how to identify the bad ideas that target us. We'll learn how to immunize ourselves with good ideas that assure us we are loved, enable us to be patient in suffering, help us find our callings, bring us into peaceful community with others, and replace despair with hope.

Yes, bad ideas are highly contagious. But they can be defeated if we keep one simple thing in mind.

HOW BAD IDEAS ARE DEFEATED

The key to achieving victory in the battle of ideas is to develop a worldview we can affirm and embrace every day until it becomes a habit. As Aristotle said, habit is what brings virtue to completion.[3] We become the thoughts we habitually have chiseled into the granite of daily practice.

This is how Rick Rescorla became a hero. He cultivated a worldview of standing strong and never leaving anyone behind. "I don't believe in being a soft man," he said. "I believe in being a tough guy."[4] This single idea formed a pattern that he consciously followed, whether as a unit commander in the Vietnam War or as head of security for a major investment firm.

Being tough is a virtue where Rick grew up in Cornwall, England, a rural county that, on a map, looks like a dragon's tail jutting out into the Atlantic. Throngs of tourists visit the area each summer, and a few hardy ones straggle in to watch the winter waves batter the coast. But most Cornish people are there to work and work hard. They're quarry workers, fishermen, and farmers—tough people who refuse to give in to difficulty.

Cornwallians express their worldview through songs such as this historic battle hymn:

> Men of Cornwall, stop your dreaming;
> Can't you see their spearpoints gleaming?
> See their warriors' pennants streaming
> To this battlefield.

> Men of Cornwall, stand ye steady;
> It cannot be ever said ye
> For the battle were not ready;
> Stand and never yield![5]

Much of the Cornwallian worldview is wrapped up in this hymn. Bad people exist: stop pretending they don't. Get ready and never give in. Through song, Cornwallians express what is true about the world and give one another courage to face it.

Rick loved to sing songs such as this one. Often he would sneak a beer to a lonely blind resident at a nursing home, wrapping his arm around the frail man and belting out Cornish songs until tears streamed down both their faces. Rick's worldview told him that tough guys don't leave anyone behind.

Rick's valor saved many lives in Vietnam. When death seemed certain at Ia Drang, a horrifying military engagement later recounted in the book *We Were Soldiers Once ... and Young*,[6] Rick sang battle hymns to his fellow warriors as they repulsed multiple enemy attacks. Later, those men described Rick as a hero, a label he rejected. "The real heroes are dead," he said simply.[7] Rick's worldview said that tough guys just do what's right; they don't need credit.

But although Rick did not consider himself a hero, he never stopped protecting those under his care. Ultimately, he rose to become vice president of security for Morgan Stanley. From his office on the forty-fourth floor of the south tower of the World Trade Center, Rick implemented strict safety procedures. He conducted surprise evacuation drills, timing them with a stopwatch and confronting senior executives who griped about the interruptions.

So when Mohamed Atta steered a hijacked 767 into the ninety-third to ninety-ninth floors of the neighboring tower on September 11, 2001, the Morgan Stanley employees knew what to do. Floor wardens organized their areas. Stronger employees assisted the disabled. As they moved down a dark and smoky stairwell, Rick serenaded them, just as he had done to his troops in Vietnam. "Men of Cornwall, stand ye steady," he sang through his bullhorn. "Stand and never yield!"

The events of 9/11 made Rick a hero. All but six of Morgan Stanley's nearly twenty-seven hundred employees based in the World Trade Center complex survived, including Deanna Williamson. And though she doesn't know for certain, Deanna believes that the woman she assisted in descending the stairway also made it.

Once his evacuees were safe, Rick called his wife, Susan. "If something should happen to me, I want you to know I've never been happier. You made my life."[8] Those were the final words he spoke to her. Rick was last seen in the tower's stairwell at the tenth floor, heading back *up* to rescue more people. A few minutes after he was spotted climbing the stairs, the skyscraper collapsed. Rick's body was never recovered.

Journalist Michael Grunwald described Rick's death as "one of those inspirational hero-tales that have sprouted like wildflowers from the Twin Towers rubble."[9] But this telling misses a crucial part of the story. Rick's heroism was a lifetime in the making. The ideas he had cultivated his whole life had formed into habit. Lifesaving action became a reflex.

Like Rick, we can develop a worldview that gives us something to live by—and something to live for. We can form a worldview that functions like an immune system and wards off the bad ideas that make us miserable. This is important because bad viruses can't be conquered with good viruses. There is no "good" cold that combats the virus that causes a bad cold. Preachers and politicians and philosophers can't live out our worldviews for us. It's time for each of us to step up.

FIVE DECLARATIONS OF FREEDOM

Through decades of military service and security work, Rick had learned to spot threats. When the first jet struck the north tower, many at first assumed it was the tragic result of mechanical or navigational failure. But Rick knew better. His worldview was straightforward. America's enemies wanted to destroy the World Trade Center, and now they had done it. This was the new normal. As a tough guy, Rick was determined to help as many people as possible survive the attack.

My life revolves around boosting the power of good ideas and blunting the effects of bad ones. Through a program called the Summit, I help prepare people of all ages to strengthen their Christian worldview and become leaders. Once my students tune in to the world of ideas, they can see the way bad ideas fill their hearts and minds with wrong answers to life's biggest questions. In the end, most of them learn to trust what God has revealed about himself, the world, and humanity. I have seen the Summit change thousands of lives.

As a graduate of the Summit myself and now as its CEO, I have lived in the world of ideas, receiving bachelor's, master's, and doctoral degrees from leading universities. Decades of reading, studying, and interacting with others have led me to believe that some of the ideas to which I have been exposed are genuine and some are counterfeit. I have studied secularism, Marxism, postmodernism, new spirituality, and Islam, among other worldviews. I have learned that some idea viruses are crafted in primitive training camps. Others are assembled on prestigious college campuses, in distinguished-looking legislative chambers, in libraries, or even in buildings covered with religious symbols.

Knowing a little about how viruses work has helped me prepare students to develop a simple set of good ideas based on what Jesus taught and deftly counter the attacks of bad ideas. Long experience shows me that our deepest heart questions revolve around love, hurt, meaning, peace, and hope. Here's a simple set of "declarations of freedom"—five truths that release us from the grip of idea viruses that intend to do us harm. These declarations help us get a proper view *of* the world and *for* the world and resist the bad ideas trying to penetrate our defenses:

1. **I am loved.** Deep, unconditional love exists, and I can have it.
2. **My suffering will be overcome.** Hurt will not win. Indeed, it already has lost.
3. **I have an incredible calling.** My life has meaning. I bear God's image.
4. **I am meant for community.** I can overcome conflict and live at peace with those around me.
5. **There is hope for the world.** I am not doomed. What is right and just and true will win.

In *The Secret Battle of Ideas of God*, we'll see that these declarations of freedom are not just positive self-talk. They have deep roots in the teachings of Jesus and his culture. Nor are they theological platitudes. They're very practical and livable. That's the good news.

But the bad news is that these declarations are under attack. Bad ideas flood our minds and hearts every day, trying to convince us that love isn't real, that suffering is meaningless, that our lives have no purpose, that we are all alone, and that despair is our lot. Bad ideas are on the attack. We need a strong worldview to keep them at bay.

Keeping viruses at bay is what researchers do at places such as the United States Army Medical Research Institute of Infectious Diseases (USAMRIID; pronounced u-SAM-rid) at Fort Detrick, near Frederick, Maryland. It was there on November 17, 1989, that two researchers working in a biohazard lab peered into a microscope. They stared at what could have been the worst disaster to ever land on American soil.

Curious about why so many monkeys had been dying at a nearby medical-research facility, the researchers had ground up one of the deceased primates' spleens and let it sit over the week. This Friday before Thanksgiving, they couldn't resist coming in for a look before their break.

They instantly regretted their choice.

CHAPTER 2

STOPPING BAD IDEAS

Four Things to Do When You're on the Brink of the Apocalypse

Researchers at USAMRIID study every imaginable infectious disease. They thought they had seen it all, but never had they encountered anything like this. Looking through a microscope, they saw monkey cells collapsing. Melting, almost.

The cause was a killer virus: nearly all the monkeys that were exposed to it died.[1] What worried the researchers even more was that the deadly virus had spread through the air. Monkeys had been isolated from one another in separate cages and still contracted the deadly disease.

What if humans were susceptible?[2] The two researchers looked at each other. The virus, known as Ebola, could represent an apocalypse. And it wasn't half a world away in some remote region. The caged monkeys were warehoused in an office park in Reston, Virginia. That's thirty minutes outside Washington, DC.

BAD IDEAS CAN KILL YOU

Viruses can kill on a mass scale. Take the horrific Spanish flu outbreak, for example. In 1918 and 1919, it killed an estimated fifty million people worldwide.[3] According to the National Archives and Records Administration, "In one year, the average life expectancy in the United States dropped by 12 years."[4] And today, because of air travel and continued mass movements of people, researchers worry that a similar outbreak might encircle the globe in days rather than years.[5] That's what happened in 2009 when swine flu was detected in Mexico. Within a week, it had spread to the United Kingdom.[6]

Ideas spread even faster. Through social media, they can travel the world in nanoseconds. At this moment, every "ism" from every part of the world—from communism to terrorism to material-ism—is recruiting followers right here, among people who have backgrounds and outward lifestyles very similar to our own.

Think modern medicine will save you from killer viruses? Think again. Scientists do their best, of course, but effective vaccines can take from four months to fifteen years to develop. By then, a deadly contagion might have claimed millions of victims.

The twentieth century shows that ideas can be just as deadly. During two world wars, earth's most powerful nations slaughtered one another. Most of those killed were noncombatants: tens of millions of civilians shot, gassed, bombed, or killed by war-related starvation and disease.

Both of those wars began as wars of ideas. Looking back on World War II, we can see how Nazism in Germany, fascism in Italy, and imperialism in Japan were ideas that led nations to terrorize and kill millions. But the Russian Communists, who seemed cooperative with the other Allied powers, also were maneuvering behind the scenes to overthrow entire governments, economic structures, and cultures. Somewhere between 80 million and 100 million people have been killed by Communist governments, making it the most brutal form of government ever devised by humanity.[7]

The world took its stand against Nazism, fascism, and Japanese imperialism, but communism's death toll was perhaps ten times greater than that of Nazi Germany.

Whereas Nazism, fascism, and imperialism were based on an exaggerated sense of national pride, Marxism was an intellectual movement. It was modernism's first truly complete worldview, carefully crafted in a library by the unkempt social misfit Karl Marx. It gave an account of everything from psychology and sociology to politics and economics. For sixty-nine years after the publication of the *Communist Manifesto* in 1848, communism reproduced in fertile minds. Its first major outbreak, the October Revolution in Russia in 1917, forever reshaped the world.

Marxism isn't the only worldview reproducing itself in millions of minds, reshaping the world. In addition to Marxism, we'll look at five other worldviews in the chapters that follow.

When faced with potentially catastrophic viral outbreaks, scientists have learned not to sit back and hope for the best. Rather, they take decisive action, using four specific steps to curb a virus's growing impact. Will these same four steps help us counteract the bad ideas that threaten humanity?

HOW TO STOP VIRUSES BEFORE THEY SPREAD OUT OF CONTROL

Fortunately for the USAMRIID researchers—and for America— the Reston Ebola virus of 1989 turned out not to be fatal to humans. But the scientists knew that America had come frighteningly close to a deadly outbreak.

Some African countries have not been so fortunate. In 2014, a ruinous Ebola outbreak occurred in the desperately poor African nation of Guinea. A critical-care physician named Rob Fowler traveled to Guinea to offer his help, knowing this could be a death sentence. He arrived at the Kipe Hospital in Conakry, where doctors and nurses—the frontline defense against the Ebola virus—had been infected with the disease they were trying to fight.

Fowler saw few others receiving care at the hospital. "Where are the patients?" he asked.

"They ran away," he was told.[8]

A rumor had spread that people were dying because doctors were killing them. Fearful and feverish, the patients had returned home. In doing this, they signed their own death warrants and those of their family members. Some 3,800 people in Guinea came down with Ebola. More than 2,500 of them died.[9]

Viral outbreaks are frustratingly hard to stop. Viruses aren't alive and thus can't really die. And viruses are everywhere, with new ones being discovered all the time.[10] Not only that but they're also incredibly compact, undetectable except through the use of advanced microscopes. Some viruses, such as polio, are so tiny that millions of them could fit inside the period at the end of this sentence.[11]

Viruses enter the body through small cuts as well as through the eyes, nose, and mouth. Once in a person's system, they take cells hostage and reproduce rapidly. When a person has the flu, his or her cells might have churned out one hundred trillion virus copies.[12] Fortunately, when alerted to their presence, the immune system goes into action isolating infected cells. The sick person gets better in a few days.

Viruses such as Ebola, however, are more difficult for the body to deal with because they shut off its alarm system and reproduce themselves without being detected. By the time it bursts into the bloodstream, Ebola is almost impossible to stop. The body responds by storming in with all its immune-system weapons blazing in what is called a cytokine storm.[13] This seriously undermines the virus's work, but it also causes collateral damage. Blood vessels begin leaking. Clotting agents try to stem the leakage, but this only prevents blood from reaching vital organs. Blood pressure drops. The body goes into shock. Death looms.

Stopping viruses such as Ebola seems impossible, but it's not. Learning from Ebola's first outbreaks in Africa, in which most of the victims died, the medical community has dramatically increased the survival rate. Thousands died in the most recent outbreak, but millions more might have if scientists had not responded so decisively with four steps:

1. Scientists *identified* the virus's characteristics.
2. Scientists *isolated* the virus's impact by tracing where it had been and who was at risk.
3. Scientists *informed* people of how to stop the virus.
4. Scientists *invested* in those who were sick by helping their bodies survive and recover.[14]

Let's look at how these four steps—identify, isolate, inform, and invest—can help us arrest the influence of bad ideas just as they help curb the effect of deadly viruses before they do irreversible harm to us and those we love.

FOUR STEPS TO ARRESTING THE INFLUENCE OF BAD IDEAS

Thinking of bad ideas as viruses can help us see how ideas work. It also can help us stop bad ideas from attacking us and those we love. Let's see if the four steps that stop viruses can help stop bad ideas from succeeding in their miserable onslaught.

STEP 1: IDENTIFY

Doctors can identify viruses by the symptoms they cause: aches and pains, fever, and so forth. This is true of ideas too. Among Christians, for example, a terrible "virus" is striking the young.

They are walking away from their faith. One measure of this virus's reach is how many drop out of church. Up to 75 percent of students who were significantly involved in church in high school are no longer even attending church as twentysomethings, and only 35 percent return and attend regularly (defined as at least twice a month).[15] Many blame higher education. But those who don't attend college after high school are even *more* likely than college-goers to curb their church attendance.[16]

What kinds of bad ideas produce such casualties? Having worked with hundreds of thousands of young adults, I've come to believe they fall prey to one of five worldviews:

- **Secularism. Life is about control.** We can use our intelligence to harness evolution and make life turn out the way we want. I'll call this worldview *secularism*, from a Latin word meaning "life span." Secularists don't ask what God wants or what history requires of us but instead what we think best serves us during our lifetimes.

- **Marxism. Life is about capital.** As we saw earlier, Karl Marx in the mid-1800s proposed that the working class's wretched condition was due to exploitation by the rich. Whereas the Bible directs believers to work hard and share with those in need, *Marxism* demands a forcible overthrow of all existing social structures: government, the economy, religion, and family.[17]

- **Postmodernism. Life is about context.**
  According to this worldview, "capital *T*"
  truth cannot be known to exist; there are only
  "lowercase *t*" truths that we create for ourselves.
  We need to be "post"-modern, this worldview
  argues, investing our time uncovering the ways
  religious and scientific people try to trick us into
  thinking they're right. This is *postmodernism*.

- **New spirituality. Life is about consciousness.** With new spirituality, at the core of
  reality is a higher consciousness, a force some
  people call "god." Spirituality isn't just *a* thing;
  it is the *only* thing. Whereas King David in
  Psalm 119:48 wrote about meditating on
  God's words, new spirituality recommends
  spiritual practices that make people feel at one
  with the universe.[18]

- **Islam. Life is about conquering.** A sixth-
  century nomad named Muhammad claimed
  that an angel revealed humanity's need to
  unite around sincere worship of one God:
  Allah, in Arabic. Considering itself to be
  the one true religion, Islam teaches that we
  all are born Muslim ("those who submit").
  Disbelief must be conquered through *jihad*.

Each of these worldviews—secularism, Marxism, post-modernism, new spirituality, and Islam—says something about God, existence, right versus wrong, life, the soul, society, governance, law, money, and history.[19] But how do these five worldviews fare in answering our deep heart questions about love, healing, meaning, peace, and hope?

How each worldview tries to answer life's most profound questions is what we will explore in *The Secret Battle of Ideas about God*. We'll also look at a sixth worldview, which I'll describe in a moment. Because ideas form into worldviews, we always have clues to where they've been and where they're going, like a jet's vapor trail across the sky.

STEP 2: ISOLATE

After identifying bad ideas, we have to look at how they spread so we can stop them. Airline agents sometimes ask a passenger, "Has anyone you don't know given you anything to carry aboard this aircraft?" I always say no, but it doesn't occur to me that I could in fact be hosting millions of lethal pathogens. Many people carrying viruses don't display symptoms themselves. They're not sick in any noticeable way, but they can make others sick with every touch. This is why we need to look at patterns of how symptoms break out, not just individual cases.

The same is true of the ways bad ideas are spread. They hitch rides on someone or something that otherwise seems completely harmless. Just as viruses trick the body because they're coated with

proteins, something the body finds beneficial, bad ideas attempt
to make themselves believable by coating lies in bits of truth. For
example:

- *The physical world is all we can see; therefore,
  anything spiritual is merely a creation of the
  human imagination.*
- *Some rich people are greedy; therefore, we are
  justified in confiscating wealth.*
- *Often religious people lie; therefore, no religious
  message should be believed.*
- *Forces are at work beyond what we can see; therefore, God must be a force, not a person.*
- *People rebel against God; therefore, they should be
  forced to submit.*

Bad ideas masquerade as something good—or at least harmless. Otherwise, they wouldn't spread. You probably wouldn't be
tricked by an idea that explicitly promotes fear, disappointment,
despair, or defeat.

Because they give *some* truth but not the *whole* truth, bad
ideas are like counterfeits. Once when I was traveling in a large
city overseas, a man sidled up to me and asked, "Hey, would you
like a real fake Rolex?" I don't think he understood the nuance. A
real fake is fake—*fake* fake is a double negative, which means it is
real. Plainly, his watches were not real; they were just very cleverly
constructed counterfeits.

Counterfeit worldviews look and sound like the real thing. Their labels say they are genuine. But when you buy them, you don't get what you pay for.

STEP 3: INFORM

William McGuire, a psychology professor in the 1950s, specialized in showing people how to resist bad ideas. He suggested that you don't just tell people the truth; you also inform them about the lies that would stand against the truth. You give them a little of the disease so they can build an immunity to it. It's called inoculation. Inoculation seemed to work against deadly viruses such as polio and smallpox. McGuire thought it might also help people resist bad ideas.[20]

To test his theory, McGuire prepared arguments in favor of widely rejected claims such as "Brushing your teeth is bad for you." He organized participants into groups. Members of the groups had the benefit of varying levels of preparation, from none at all to a complex mix of exposure, counterargument, and preparation to refute claims that would be made.[21]

As you might expect, better-prepared participants were less likely to be caught off guard. But one disturbing finding emerged: just reinforcing what people already knew seemed to make them *more* susceptible to bad ideas.

How can it be that reinforcing a person's preexisting opposition to a foreign idea is worse than doing nothing? Let's say that all your life you'd been told the story of Noah's ark. In Sunday school you even colored an ark with crayons as you sang about animals going in two by two. But then you got to college and found your professors proposing foreign ideas about Noah's ark. "There is no evidence of a global flood," one might have said. "Can you imagine a God so heartless as to let innocent people drown?" another might have asked. Just by their skepticism you might have concluded that intelligent people see the story of Noah's ark as a crazy myth that only ancient people, who did not know any better, believed. If no one had ever prepared you to respond to such points but just told the Noah story over and over again, you might begin seeing your Sunday school teacher as holding childish beliefs that should be rejected.

The point is that we can't just pretend bad ideas don't exist or hope no one will believe them. It seems counterintuitive, but with so many bad ideas threatening to infect us, focusing on only what we know to be true doesn't build up the immunity we need. Even the strongest of us is vulnerable.

STEP 4: INVEST

The final thing you can do to stop bad ideas is help people survive once they've been attacked. With Ebola, doctors treat patients through medication to combat infection and with massive doses of fluids and electrolytes to keep the body from going into shock.[22] Prompt intervention buys time for the body to fight for itself, increasing the chance of survival.

It's true with idea viruses too. You can't "uninfect" someone. But you can help him fight off the infectious ideas by dialoguing about them:

- "Would you be willing to tell me what you're thinking?"
- "I just want you to know I love you and am cheering for you to find good answers."
- "Have you considered …?"
- "May I share something I've learned that has helped me a lot?"

Love. Encourage. Administer truth in doses appropriate to what the person can handle.

For the remainder of this book, we'll *identify* and *isolate* how the five counterfeit worldviews attempt to answer deep heart questions such as the following: Am I loved? Why do I hurt? Does my life have meaning? Why can't we all get along? Is there hope for the world? Then with each question, we'll examine how a sixth worldview *informs* and *invests* in humanity to create health and wholeness.

A SIXTH WORLDVIEW THAT PROVIDES THE CURE

The sixth worldview we'll look at is the Christian worldview. It says that life is about Jesus Christ. This isn't a religious claim; it's about the simple premise that Jesus answers life's toughest questions when other worldviews leave us unfulfilled.

According to the Christian worldview, the other five worldviews—secularism, Marxism, postmodernism, new spirituality, and Islam—offer interesting insights. However, the battle among

competing worldviews is not like a sports league, in which theoreti-
cally evenly matched teams compete for the championship. Rather,
says the Christian worldview, there is *a* way, *a* truth, and *a* path to
the good life. As respected theologian and Anglican priest John Stott
said, "Christ is the centre of Christianity; all else is circumference."[23]

Jesus claimed to be the way, truth, and life (see John 14:6).
Often this has been understood as trusting Jesus to save us from
hell. In this book, though, we'll consider the possibility that Jesus
doesn't just offer the true way to avoid death; he offers a way
to think as he thinks and feel what he feels about finding love,
healing hurt, discovering meaning, pursuing peace, and living
with hope.

The first of life's big questions that we'll explore is this: Am I
really loved for who I am and not just what people want from me?
As we search for love, idea viruses wait in the wings, promising love
but delivering only selfishness, abuse, and even hate. Our need for
love can make us susceptible to just about anything. As we will see
in the next chapter, no one knows this more than those who recruit
for the world's worst terrorist organization.

CHAPTER 3

AM I LOVED?

How Idea Viruses Make Us Feel
Unappreciated, Unwanted, and Alone

Alex was twenty-three years old and a Sunday school teacher. Desperately lonely, she just wanted someone to care about her. That's when terrorists found her.

As a toddler, Alex had been taken from her drug-addicted mother and given to her grandparents. As a young adult, she had few friends and spent most of her time streaming Netflix and checking her social-media accounts. After reading an article about a horrific beheading committed by ISIS, Alex posted a critical comment online. A young Syrian ISIS fighter replied.

Alex was shocked and curious. She wrote back. The two began Skyping. Soon after, an ISIS recruiter named Faisal got in touch with Alex. He even sent gifts to her home.

Faisal told her that ISIS's only goal was establishing a homeland where Muslims could be more faithful in worshipping God.

He spent hours on social media responding to Alex's questions, listening, and identifying with her sadness and loneliness.

Receiving this level of focused attention wore down Alex's resistance. She stopped listening to Christian music and began playing ISIS anthems on her smartphone. She began to fantasize about escaping her boring life and joining ISIS fighters in their cause.

In the end, Alex converted to Islam. "I actually have brothers and sisters," she posted on social media. "I'm crying."[1] But surprisingly, when Alex told Faisal she had found a mosque just a few miles from her home where she could meet other Muslims, he discouraged her from attending. He warned that she would be persecuted and even labeled a terrorist.

By the time her grandparents caught on, Alex was on the brink of joining ISIS. An idea virus had taken hold, convincing her that ISIS militants aren't cruel people; they are just trying to survive, like everyone else.

Lonely and under pressure, Alex didn't realize she had become a target. She didn't notice her mental alarm system switching off. She didn't grasp the subtleties of Faisal's brainwashing techniques. Middle East expert Nasser Weddady said, "All of us have a natural firewall in our brain that keeps us from bad ideas. [ISIS recruiters] look for weaknesses in the wall, and then they attack."[2]

Faisal made Alex feel wanted, even while walling her off from her own family and other Muslim converts. As Mubin Shaikh, a former recruiter for a radical Muslim group, stated straightforwardly, "We look for people who are isolated. And if they are not isolated already, then we isolated them."[3]

Ironically, though, Alex didn't feel isolated by her ISIS contacts. She cared for them and felt they cared for her. Yearning for connection, Alex opened herself to a counterfeit version of love that nearly drew her into Islam's most extreme sect.

None of us would readily admit it, but we are more like Alex than we might think. Our longing for love can open our heart's gates to a secret enemy.

HOW BAD IDEAS EXPLOIT OUR LONGING FOR LOVE

Above all else, the human heart cries out to know, *Am I loved?* We're hardwired for intimacy. A study of Romanian orphans found that lack of love early in life led to decreased brain activity.[4] Without affection, a person's language center, emotions, and ability to take in information get short-circuited, leading to lifelong problems.

Our experience with love forms our desires, our characters, and our core identities. Our love shapes our lives. We are designed to give and receive love, yet many of us feel deprived of it. Famished, our hunger for affection tempts us to settle for less than the best or put up with being mistreated or meet our sexual needs in ways we know are wrong. In the end, we're worse off than when we began.

The terrorists who targeted Alex knew she was vulnerable. They used that opening to hijack her desires in order to turn her into an ideological weapon. It's frightening to think of what might have happened if she had followed through with joining ISIS. Many recruits have become soldiers or even suicide bombers. In the secret battle of ideas, bad ideas can be deadlier than bullets.

Militant groups manipulate the human need for intimacy as a way to grow their ranks. Other worldviews might not build armies, but they're still recruiting people to help them change the world according to what they believe—or at least convincing people to stay out of the way while others do it.

If we want to find true love, we must *identify* its counterfeits and *isolate* which worldview makes us feel particularly vulnerable.

IDENTIFYING THE LIES COUNTERFEIT WORLDVIEWS TELL ABOUT LOVE

Remember this about counterfeit worldviews: they present just enough truth to get people to believe a bigger lie. This is especially true in what each worldview says about love, sex, and intimacy. Let's look at the lies, examining the secular worldview last because of its extraordinary influence.

MARXISM

Marxism argues that we can't find love because capitalists rig the system to cause us to always want more than we have. Programmed to believe we are lacking in wealth or possessions, we become easy to control. In his book *Das Kapital*, Karl Marx referred to this as the "fetishism of commodities."[5] According to Marx's editor and collaborator, Frederick Engels, this fetishism causes us to think we are fulfilled in love only when we "own" our relationships as if they were possessions. When capitalism is abolished, however, everyone will belong to everyone, leading to "unconstrained sexual intercourse" based on a "more tolerant public opinion."[6]

POSTMODERNISM

Postmodernism says we speak of love to mask what we're really after, which is sex. Yet those in power control us through guilt, making us feel ashamed for having sexual thoughts and feelings. This is especially the case if those thoughts and feelings involve same-sex attraction.[7] The solution? Explore sexuality until the guilt feelings cease. Postmodern thinker Michel Foucault led the way. A deeply troubled postmodern scholar who enjoyed ritual sexual abuse[8], Foucault advocated for creating "an ever expanding encyclopaedia of preferences, gratifications and perversions."[9] Many have followed his lead, putting sexual exploration at the heart of the search for love. This is especially true in higher education. At an age when young adults most need help in how best to love and respect others, what they get instead are classes such as Oberlin College's How to Win a Beauty Pageant and DePaul University's Deconstructing the Diva, not to mention "sex weeks" during which pornographic films are shown and safe-sex kits are distributed.[10]

NEW SPIRITUALITY

New spirituality says the universe is love. We are part of the universe. Therefore, we *are* love. If we don't feel loved, it's because we're not familiar enough with our own universal power. Said new-spiritualist writer Marianne Williamson, "Every problem, inside and out, is due to separation from love on someone's part."[11] When we reunite with universal love, we become attractive. Writer Arielle Ford illustrated this by telling of an unnamed actress who began living as if the person of her dreams were already part of her life. As she played music she thought this person might enjoy, she prepared candlelight dinners at which she set an extra place at the table for the as-yet-unidentified lover. Ford wrote, "She sent a clear message to the Universe, and the Universe delivered."[12]

ISLAM

Islam, the conquering worldview, doesn't talk a lot about love or sex, at least in Islamic sacred writings. Love is mentioned a scant sixty-nine times in the Quran, and many of the references pertain to the dangers of loving that which Allah hates. One impression comes through clearly: Allah's love must be earned by submission. Allah will love you *if* you trust him, exercise patience, and fight on his behalf. The idea that Allah *is* love is not a part of Islamic thinking. Of course, the Quran does acknowledge that people fall in love. However, it considers this to be a matter of the heart and not something of religious importance, so long as the couple doesn't violate Allah's commands governing sexual contact.

People who adhere to these worldviews—Marxism, post-modernism, new spirituality, and Islam—do not necessarily walk in lockstep with one another. But assumptions determine conclusions. What we assume to be true about the world definitely narrows the range of behavior we consider acceptable.

But even considering how influential these worldviews are in affecting how we understand and practice love, no worldview exerts a greater influence than secularism. Secularists say we don't feel loved because we haven't yet freed ourselves from society's constraints about sexuality.[13] So, can sexual freedom bring the love we crave? Whether secularism can deliver on it is another matter. My own youthful experience with sex leads me to believe that it cannot. Here's what I mean.

SURVIVAL IS ALL THERE IS TO IT: ISOLATING THE WAY THE SECULAR WORLDVIEW HIJACKS LOVE

Nothing outside the material world exists, secularism says. The Enlightenment gave birth to this viewpoint, bitterly blaming eternity-focused religions for society's ills. The Enlightenment also gave birth to Darwinism, which made it intellectually respectable to believe that humans are nothing more than complex animals, which means that restraining our impulses is unnatural. Together, these two ideas led to a revolution—a sexual revolution. Without a shot being fired, secularism forever altered what we mean when we say "I love you."

WHAT SECULARISTS MEAN WHEN THEY SAY "I LOVE YOU"

In the 1900s, psychoanalyst Sigmund Freud and sexologist Alfred Kinsey, among others, concluded that *love* is just a term we use to describe our brains' being stimulated by sexual desire. They said that because only the material world exists, no deity can prescribe what is sexually right or wrong. We control that ourselves.[14]

But the secular worldview of love isn't about sex, per se; it's about the survival of the species. Sex is part of that, along with our protective instinct for our offspring. According to secularists, a mother's saying "I love you" to a child is not an indication that the mother is trying to feed the child's soul; she's just using words to keep the child close and to enhance its chances of survival. When lovers say "I love you," they aren't making a commitment to be together no matter what. They're just describing their hormonal reactions.

Because secularism fumbles in explaining love, it also fumbles in explaining why people *don't* love—why they sometimes despise and want to harm one another. Psychologist Rollo May admitted, "Today we know a great deal about bodily chemistry and the control of physical diseases; but we know very little about why people hate, why they cannot love, why they suffer anxiety and guilt, and why they destroy each other."[15]

I understand May's admission. When I was younger, my frantic clamoring for love allowed an idea virus to take hold in my heart, leading me to destructive actions. I have hesitated to talk about those years because I came to believe that "everyone makes mistakes—just move on and don't talk about it." Idea viruses, though, leave scar tissue that affects our lives for the duration. The scars can't be hidden, so here's the story.

HOW TO GET LOST SEARCHING FOR INTIMACY

My growing-up years were mostly safe and stable. My involved and caring parents today describe themselves as having been "intellectually locked." In rearing their children, they emphasized the mind more than the heart. For most of my childhood, I knew I was cared for, but I also ached for affection. This led me to make some heartbreaking decisions that I'm still affected by today.

In my case, college offered the opportunity to find the intimacy I had desired growing up. I did find it, sexually at least. Sleeping around made me feel wanted. It enhanced my status among my fraternity brothers. And when I didn't have a partner, pornography was always available.

Rather than orient me to the truth, the college courses I took just affirmed my actions. This world is all there is, my professors implied, and if our bodies are all we have and our sexual impulses are our strongest biochemical reactions, then sexual expression is how we become real.

In seeking intimacy through sex, though, I got my girlfriend pregnant. Not wanting the responsibility of having a family, I didn't object when she floated the idea of getting an abortion. In fact, I paid half the fee. Our relationship ended soon after that. Years later, I would be brought low by this. My sexual actions had hurt a loving, kind person and ended a budding life. At the time, though, I just felt relief, as if I had somehow narrowly escaped the consequences of my actions.

But consequences are not so easily dismissed. A fear of intimacy began reproducing itself in my heart. Feeling that I might hurt someone if I got too close to them emotionally, I whipsawed between intimacy and isolation. Ultimately, I chose to be chaste until marriage. But I chose that because I was running from the problems brought on by intimacy, not because I wanted to pursue purity. I chose the right path, but for the wrong reasons.

CONSEQUENCES OF THE SECULAR WORLDVIEW'S DEFINITION OF LOVE

If exposure to sex could fulfill our craving for love, humanity should be feeling very loved by now. In the United States, 46 percent of high school students have had sex.[16] That figure rises to over 70 percent by the time students are in college.[17] This leads to both physical and emotional consequences.

Physically, sex uncoupled from lifelong commitment has created a national health nightmare. In the 1950s, there were only two significant sexually transmitted diseases—syphilis and gonorrhea—both of which were treatable with penicillin.[18] Now there are more than twenty-four, with half having no cure.[19] Nearly one-fourth of new HIV/AIDS infections occur in young people between the ages of thirteen and twenty-four.[20] More people die each year from HIV/AIDS than through homicides involving firearms or drunk driving.[21]

Emotionally, promiscuity generates a mocking twist: pursuing intimacy through sexual transactions defeats the very thing most people say they're after, which is someone to love and be loved by for a lifetime. Engaging in sex prior to marriage is closely connected to increased depression, sexual unfaithfulness, and marital disruption.[22]

Pornography makes it even worse. A Princeton University study showed that viewing pictures of scantily clad women activated the "tool use" part of men's brains, causing them to view women as objects.[23] And porn doesn't just change what people think about; it changes the anatomy and physiology of the brain itself. Neuroscientist William Struthers has said that porn is like crack cocaine, causing the brain to become neurochemically dependent.[24] This is especially startling given that more than 40 percent of the world's Internet users view porn,[25] including more than 40 percent of ten- to seventeen-year-olds.[26] We're further from finding true love than we've ever been.

Recently some buddies and I were watching football on television. During a commercial about erectile dysfunction, I cracked, "You know, I've just realized the guys in that ad are my age." The group laughed, and then a twentysomething friend spoke up: "More and more guys taking that drug are *my* age. They've used porn so much they can't get an erection when they're with a real woman." Separating love and sex is like catching a butterfly by stomping on it. It mars what is beautiful about intimacy. It also ruins sex.

Yet sex sells, no doubt about it. A study of more than three thousand magazine ads from the past thirty years found that, by 2003, nearly one out of every three ads was using sexual imagery to sell its products.[27] These messages infiltrate our hearts' immune systems like viruses. *You aren't loved,* they seem to say, *but at least you can have an orgasm and forget your aloneness for a while.* In moments of weakness, these idea viruses gain a foothold. Eventually, we're so desperate for love that, like Alex wanting to join ISIS, we might even begin defending that which we once found shocking.[28] Ideas have consequences, and scientific advancement and modern psychology haven't brought us closer to finding the love we long for.

COUNTERFEIT WORLDVIEWS LEAD TO COUNTERFEIT LOVE

Shakespeare wrote in *Romeo and Juliet,* "Love is a smoke made with the fume of sighs."[29] When we don't have it, we pine for it. When we have it, it can be exasperating. Either way, we're never sure what it is that we really want. The Marxist and postmodernist worldviews try to clear things up by pointing out that we're being manipulated by our culture. The new spirituality worldview rightly points out that if we want to be loved, we ought to try to be lovable. The Islamic worldview says God is not pleased when we give in to wrong desires. The secular worldview astutely notes that we humans are sexual beings (duh) and that our instinct to survive has something to do with what we call love.

But when these truths get wrapped around lies, bad ideas enter our hearts and minds:

- *God doesn't love you unless you do exactly what he says.*
- *Love doesn't even exist.*
- *Forget love; have sex.*
- *Think loving thoughts and you'll find love.*
- *Stop this frivolous nonsense about love and join the revolution.*

None of these views gives us any assurance that our deep desires can be met. They're just idea viruses making us sicker.

Few people express this as well as Douglas Coupland, the novelist who popularized the term *Generation X* and a self-proclaimed cynical, angry, narcissistic, sexually broken person:

> Now—here is my secret: I tell it to you with an openness of heart that I doubt I shall ever achieve again, so I pray that you are in a quiet room as you hear these words. My secret is that I need God—that I am sick and can no longer make it alone. I need God to help me give, because I no

longer seem to be capable of giving; to help me
be kind, as I no longer seem capable of kindness; to help me love, as I seem beyond being
able to love.[30]

This is where we are—all of us. We want real love. And as we
will see in the next chapter, where it is found may well be one of
the most surprising discoveries of our lives.

CHAPTER 4

LOVE NEVER FAILS

How Jesus Meets Our Hearts' Deepest Longings

DECLARATION: I AM LOVED. DEEP, UNCONDITIONAL LOVE EXISTS, AND I CAN HAVE IT.

Every parent knows the feeling. When you hold your child for the first time, your whole understanding of love changes. You're ready to sacrifice everything, and sometimes you do: sleep, freedom, your savings account. In a wonderful irony, the more a parent sacrifices, the more he or she loves.

It's this indescribable feeling of love that makes the thought of losing a child unbearable. Linda White has lived with this nightmare for the past thirty years. In 1986, her daughter, Cathy, was a twenty-six-year-old mother pregnant with her second child. Cathy stopped to offer help to two fifteen-year-old boys whose car had quit on them. The boys accepted her offer of a ride. Then they raped her and shot her four times, leaving her body in a field near a dirt road.

Linda was overcome with grief and anger. "I didn't see [the boys] as humans at that time," she recalls. "I was pleased when they both were sentenced to long terms in prison." But then she adds, "I feel different today."[1] Somehow Linda's grief was transformed into a kind of love that counterfeit worldviews are at a loss to explain, a love so profound that Linda forgave her daughter's killers and, in the process, brought hope to thousands.

It took a long time. At first, Linda and her husband joined victim-support groups. But they found scant comfort there. "Nobody moved, everyone stayed the same," Linda told a reporter for the BBC. "I didn't want to be five years down the road and be the way they were—full of bitterness."[2] Finally, Linda asked to meet in person with her daughter's murderers. The prison allowed her and her eighteen-year-old grand-daughter, Ami, to meet with one of the two young men. The encounter was filmed and used in a documentary called *Meeting with a Killer*.

The murderer's name is Gary Brown. Linda was astonished at how young and vulnerable he looked. She learned that he had been abused and neglected early in life. In their meeting, he expressed total remorse and offered no excuses for his crimes. She describes the encounter as "incredibly healing."[3]

During the meeting, Linda showed Gary photos of her daughter, Cathy. Cathy's daughter, Ami, talked about her struggles growing up without her mother. They told Gary, according to Mark Obbie of *Slate*, "that his resolve to live a better life is the only atonement he can make and all that they ask of him."[4]

How could Linda go through with such an excruciating meeting? She said simply, "I strongly believe that most of my journey over the last 23 years has been through grace. Otherwise, I have no explanation for it."[5]

Gary Brown was released from prison in 2010, having served twenty-three years of a fifty-four-year sentence. Linda said he became a remarkably different person, "proof that young people, even those who have done horrible things, can be transformed."[6]

Gary changed, but Linda did too. She declared freedom from the idea viruses that chained her to hate. Rather than hate, she chose to love. She became an advocate of what is called restorative justice, which helps victims find peace and gives offenders a chance to try to make things right. Linda's story illustrates how a Christian worldview transforms love itself, bringing good into the world even through a dark story of personal loss. How it does this is one of the most remarkable stories ever told.

BE INFORMED: "AGAPE" AS THE CHRISTIAN WORLDVIEW RESPONSE TO FEELING UNLOVED AND ALONE

Here are two insights, based on who the Bible reveals God to be, under which we can take shelter when we feel unloved and alone. These insights help us see that we are loved and that deep, unconditional love exists and we can have it.

INSIGHT #1: LOVE RESTS ON TWO PILLARS

Try to put yourself in the place of Linda White. Her reaching out to her daughter's murderer seems miraculous. That's because it is. A Christian worldview supernaturally transforms love by revealing two things about God that we could not grasp on our own.

First, God is a person, not a force. If God were a force, then "he" would be an "it." An "it" cannot love you. But God cares *personally*. His love, Deuteronomy tells us, is like a wall that surrounds us so we can dwell in safety (see Deut. 33:12). And it never stops. The prophet Jeremiah affirmed this message from God: "I have loved you with an everlasting love" (Jer. 31:3).

Second, God expresses his love through his presence. Unlike other ancient religions, the temple of God's chosen people contained no statue of God because *God himself* was present. In fact, the Christian worldview teaches he is present *everywhere*. Saint Paul told a group of religious scholars in Athens that the living God does not live in temples made with human hands. *We* don't give life to *him*; *he* gives life to *us* (see Acts 17:24–25).

God is personal. God is present. On these two pillars rests a deep kind of love that is hard to express in a day when we employ the word *love* to mean both our love of a favorite television show or a steak dinner and the love we have for our family and best friends. But when Jesus revealed what kind of love God expresses, the world changed forever.

INSIGHT #2: GOD'S LOVE IS SELFLESS LOVE

Unlike the language we use today, the ancient language of Koine (COIN-ay) Greek, the dialect that was used to write down Jesus's words, specifies different types of love by giving each type its own word. Love of family is *philos* (think of Philadelphia, the city of brotherly love). The word for romantic or sexual love is *eros*. But the Bible uses a third, less common word to describe the kind of love that comes from God. It's the word *agape* (ah-GAHP-ay). Agape love is a selfless, self-giving love.[7]

Everyone knows that God loved the world enough to give his only Son, as John 3:16 says. It's the most famous verse in the Bible. But through his letters, Saint Paul clarified what it looks like for *us* to love that way. He wrote, "Love [agape] is patient and kind; love [agape] does not envy or boast; it is not arrogant or rude…. Love [agape] bears all things, believes all things, hopes all things, endures all things" (1 Cor. 13:4–5, 7). Agape love comes from God, Paul said, and God is the one who pours it into our hearts by his Holy Spirit (see Rom. 5:5).

Agape love is selfless love. As we receive it from God and give it to others, our hearts' immune system grows strong against idea viruses that make us feel unloved and unloving.

HOW JESUS DEFEATS IDEA VIRUSES THAT LEAVE US FEELING UNLOVED

Linda White did not invest her love for her murdered daughter in an ongoing effort to heap greater punishment on the murderers. Rather, she used it to forgive. It's hard to explain this in purely human terms. In fact, the dominant counterfeit worldviews of our day move us further from love rather than closer to it.

Consider the way various worldviews wage the secret battle of ideas about love. Secularism, by teaching that only the material world exists, turns love into slang for the human instinct to protect family members. Secularism also attempts to explain why our need for love is so strong by equating it with sexual desire. When someone says, "Don't impose your morality on me" or "Repressing your sexual desire is dangerous," he or she has been influenced by secular idea viruses.

Other worldviews offer their own confused messages about love. Marxism says love can't exist until society's institutions are overthrown through revolution. Postmodernism denies that such a thing as love can exist. New spirituality says love comes only through tapping into the universe's power. To Islam, obedience—rather than being loved by our Creator and Redeemer and loving others—lies at the center of our religious duty.

Think of all the idea viruses these worldviews produce:

- *God does not love you; he's not even real.*
- *Love doesn't mean anything; it's all about sexual urges.*

- *Life is survival of the fittest; focus on your own needs.*
- *It's dangerous to repress your sexual desires; we're all just animals anyway.*
- *How can it be wrong if it feels so right?*
- *Only you know what is best for you.*

The list is endless.

The Christian worldview stands in contrast to these views because of Jesus. He is proof that God is personal and present; through him, God became flesh and lived among us (see John 1:14). You want to know where love is? He's right here. Eating. Drinking. Walking. Weeping. Conversing. Healing. Other gods rule through fear, taking the lives of others. Jesus overcame fear and gave his own life. There is no other God like this.

The selfless love Jesus taught is bigger than we could come up with on our own. Through traumatic life experiences, I've learned three things about selfless love. First, it meets the deep need for intimacy. Second, it grows through giving rather than getting. And finally, it tames self-love.

SELFLESS LOVE MEETS OUR NEED FOR INTIMACY

It was a marriage-counseling session, and it wasn't going well. I could barely contain my panic. As the therapist asked us to complete exercises such as writing down our top five emotional needs, I tried to humor him. "Respect. Sense of purpose," I wrote. "Peace. Feeling needed."

Then I hesitated. Finally, I wrote "Intimacy." What I really wanted to write was "Sex," but the word *intimacy* seemed more, shall we say, appropriate.

When we were finished, the counselor asked me to read my list aloud. I did. There was a long pause. "Do you need to be married to meet these needs?" he queried.

I was quite sure I did, knowing what I meant by intimacy.

"Which of these needs are you turning to your wife to meet rather than to God?"

The word *intimacy* stared back at me, burning a hole in the protective layer shielding my deepest doubts. "There is no way God can meet my need for intimacy," I said.

"Why not?"

"Because …" I said, pausing in the hope that a good rationale would come to mind. It didn't. "Okay, what about sex? How am I supposed to experience intimacy with … God? That sounds weird."

The therapist was quiet for a moment. "I don't think it's my place to convince you," he said. "Why don't you take some time tonight to explore what the Bible says?"

I nodded, but I suspected that my sexual needs were purely physical. God couldn't meet them. That night, though, after a couple hours of sleeplessness on the couch, I opened my laptop and Googled, "How can God meet my deepest needs for intimacy?" Evidently, a lot of people have wrestled with this already. Lists of Bible verses popped up. I spent much of the night looking them up.

When you're drowning, a well-placed life preserver is a thing of beauty. That's what the Bible was for me. As if for the first time,

I realized that God cares for me (see 1 Pet. 5:7). He rejoices over me with singing (see Zeph. 3:17). He will never leave me (see Heb. 13:5). Nothing can separate me from his love (see Rom. 8:39).

I could never have imagined God's meeting my deepest needs for intimacy. When my life spun out of control, though, I began understanding that he is the only one who ever could. It is intimacy with God, not my sex drive, that forms my core identity.

Still, receiving God's selfless love is not easy. It requires something of me that I find very difficult. It asks me to change from being a "getter" to being a "giver."

SELFLESS LOVE GROWS THROUGH GIVING RATHER THAN GETTING

In *The World, the Flesh, and Father Smith*, Bruce Marshall's Father Smith character meets a famous author of erotica who claims that religion is a substitute for sex. Father Smith says, "I still prefer to believe that sex is a substitute for religion and that the young man who rings the bell at the brothel is unconsciously looking for God."[8]

Father Smith nails it. We long for God but have been infected by idea viruses that tell us that *getting* rather than *giving* is the source of true love. Lots of smart people believe this. Billionaire investor Warren Buffett told a college audience that the only thing that matters in life is being loved by the people you want to have love you.[9] It sounds good on the surface, but think who the object of this love is. It's the self. It says, "*I* want to be loved by the people *I* want to have love *me*."

Acts 20:35 says we are more blessed when we give rather than receive. Buffett, viewing love as a means to an end, misses this blessing. To Jesus, love isn't a means to an end. It *is* the end. It's also the starting point and the journey itself.

This isn't just religious talk. Selfless love changes how we live on a very practical level. A study of older adults who attend church found a significant difference between those who go to church to *give*—for example, through serving, providing meals, or teaching—and those who go to church to *get*—for example, friendship, inspiration, or to fulfill a religious duty. The givers had a greater sense of purpose. They even lived longer—five years longer, on average, if this study is to be believed—than the getters.[10]

Giving selflessly changes others. One business I started several years ago trained people as mentors. Wanting to be sure we had a strong research basis, I examined more than a hundred studies that explored the influence of selfless giving. One study found that when mentors spent time with at-risk students, those students significantly decreased their bullying behavior and reported lower feelings of depression.[11] A forty-year study in Hawaii showed that protective factors like the support of an adult role model helped 50 to 80 percent of those in an at-risk population reach positive outcomes for their lives.[12]

The Christian worldview calls us to invest in others, not because they've been found to be fit to survive or because they can help spark a revolution or because it makes us feel at one with the universe or because God will punish us if we don't help them. We need to invest in them because selfless love is the only way to change hearts—theirs and our own.

SELFLESS LOVE IS STRONG ENOUGH TO TAME SELF-LOVE

Counterfeit worldviews have a hard time explaining why Linda White reached out to her daughter's killer. The Christian worldview doesn't. Jesus said, "Love your enemies, do good to those who hate you, bless those who curse you, pray for those who mistreat you" (Luke 6:27–28 NASB). Through Jesus, love transforms us, just as it did Linda when she loved Gary Brown instead of demanding vengeance.

Today, though, scholars say the epidemic of self-love is growing as fast as the obesity epidemic.[13] Marketers exploit this epidemic, telling us we "deserve" what they're selling: a new car, a Caribbean vacation, or even just a hamburger. Therapists draw on a Greek myth about a boy who fell in love with his own reflection: they use the term *narcissism* to describe self-love. Narcissists demand that we advance their interests at our own expense. They become angry when they don't get their way. They carry out hidden agendas that harm the reputation and relationships of those around them.

In a viral attack, a cytokine storm unleashes all of the immune system's weapons, often injuring the body by the way it attacks the infection. Similarly, narcissism releases all of the mind's weapons to fight off everything that it fears will not advance its own interests, leaving destruction in its wake. Even while proclaiming a love for humanity, the esteemed Enlightenment philosopher Jean-Jacques Rousseau abandoned all five of his children to orphanages, where their chances of survival were remote. Karl Marx decried bourgeoisie exploitation of women but destroyed his relationship with his loving wife by impregnating their housekeeper.[14] The promoters of the sexual revolution likewise jumped from affair to affair, breaking hearts and destroying trust along the way.

At the height of his power, Israel's warrior-poet King David was probably a narcissist. He praised friendship through flowing verse but seduced a loyal friend's wife and had his cuckolded friend killed. But David then departed from the pattern of a narcissist. When confronted with his sin, David repented and asked God to create a clean heart and renew a right spirit in him (see Ps. 51). From that point forward, he was a man after God's own heart, living to please God.

Like David, we were made to be lovers. But, as political philosopher and pastor Dale Kuehne states, "To become the lovers we are meant to be, we need to dwell in the love of God."[15] When we dwell in God's love, self-love is transformed into selfless love.

INVEST IN YOURSELF AND OTHERS: FIVE THINGS YOU CAN DO RIGHT NOW TO EXPERIENCE LOVE

A Christian worldview says our need for personal intimacy is met at its deepest level through a cosmic love story penned by the Creator of the universe.[16] It calls us to do many things differently.

1. Experience forgiveness and offer it. If Jesus can forgive the thief on the cross, he can forgive you. And you can forgive others. Selfless love relaxes our drive to figure out what we get in return. God meets our needs, so we just go ahead and love. Linda White sacrificed her "right" to see her daughter's murder avenged in the punishment of the killer. She instead chose love and grace over vengeance. She eventually came to see the murderer as human. Her selfless love gave him hope that he could change.

2. Let God take care of the timing. In my work with young adults, I've found that many make frantic decisions about things such as dating relationships. They are in a hurry to put an end to their feelings of loneliness. Selfless love shows us that no person can ultimately meet our deepest needs for intimacy. Only God can. First we accept God's unconditional love, and then we focus on giving love to others rather than using people to get the love we want.

3. Don't just give to others what they want from you. Loving selflessly doesn't mean being a doormat. If someone is hurting themselves and others, it's not loving to enable them. Notre Dame sociologist Christian Smith has said love is "self-expenditure for the genuine good of others."[17] Selfless love does what is *right* for others. It interrupts their obsession with getting, just as Christ interrupts ours.

4. Be chaste. *Chastity* is an old-fashioned term that most people think means saying no to sex. It actually means saying yes to sex, but within the boundaries of God's design. When Harvard professor Armand Nicholi asked students who were Christian converts to describe their sexual relationships before conversion, they said they were unsatisfactory both sexually and emotionally.[18] Although biblical standards of chastity seemed strict, Nicholi wrote, Christian converts "found these clear-cut boundaries less confusing than no boundaries at all and helpful in relating to members of the opposite sex 'as persons rather than sexual objects.'"[19]

5. Stay focused on God's perspective. In God's economy, we receive when we give. A study of prospective teachers who chose to work with at-risk children found that when they were given the opportunity to mentor the children personally, their sensitivity to at-risk children, and to children as individuals, grew. Further, the teachers improved their ability to cope with difficult situations.[20] When giving is hard, ask God to make clear to you how *he* sees the situation. God thinks long term and doesn't meet every desire, sometimes on purpose. Unmet desires remind us, as C. S. Lewis wrote, that we were made for another world.[21]

ONE MORE THING

Because of God's selfless love for us, each of us can make this declaration of freedom: *I am loved. Deep, unconditional love exists, and I can have it.* Selfless love rescues us from idea viruses that make us feel lonely and inadequate. It shows us we are loved and it awakens our love for others. Linda White loved her daughter's killer Gary Brown in this way. But as we move to the next big life question—"Why do I hurt?"—we must acknowledge that forgiveness didn't end Linda's pain. She still hurt. We all do, in one way or another. Do any of the worldviews we've studied offer relief from suffering? That's the question I've been asking in a whole new way as I live through some of the most painful experiences of my life.

CHAPTER 5

WHY DO I HURT?

How Idea Viruses Fail Us in Our Suffering

"I have been unhappy in this marriage for ten years. I want out."

Panic rising, all I could think was, *This can't be happening. What will people think? Our kids will be devastated.*

I became obsessed with fixing our marriage in hopes of making the pain stop. I went to counseling, met with pastors and mentors, and read books. I begged God to heal our marriage and take away our suffering.

But the pain didn't stop. Instead, it got worse. I experienced shame in being a ministry leader who couldn't keep his marriage together. I was filled with regret over the tiniest wrongs I had committed. I felt helpless to ease my children's confusion. Added to the pain was the legal nightmare I faced.

I ached with loneliness so much that I couldn't sleep at night. Caring for my children and getting my work done seemed like insurmountable obstacles. Fun things stopped being fun. Once I arrived at a holiday party and counted twenty-seven people: thirteen couples ... and me. I felt like a balloon with the air being slowly let out.

Within weeks, my marriage slipped through my fingers like water poured from a pitcher. Within months, I was served divorce papers. Within a year, it was over.

One night I dreamed I was standing in a hallway, gazing at light that spilled from an open door at the hallway's end. *The answers I'm looking for are behind that door*, I sensed. I stepped toward it, but the hallway lengthened. I broke into a run. The faster I moved, the longer the hallway became.

I awoke to a disabling feeling of powerlessness. I had heard stories about God taking away people's difficulties. "God stepped in and now it's better than ever," I'd heard some Christians say. Not to take anything away from other people's experiences, but I thought, *I can't see that my situation will ever get better.*

If you haven't journeyed through extreme pain, you will at some point. Pain is a dominant gene in the human life experience. Disease. Betrayal. Loss. Regret. It's inescapable.

When I hurt, I find myself asking, *Where is God in this?* I read about God's great deeds performed in the past, and I look forward to an eternal future with him. But where is he now, when I am being crushed?

In the din of the secret battle of ideas, pain is a stealth attack calling into question everything we thought was true. The five counterfeit worldviews we're looking at—secularism, Marxism, postmodernism, new spirituality, and Islam—try to explain why we hurt and how to stop it. But do they help us live better lives, or are they merely idea viruses that deepen our despair? Before we look for answers, we need to grapple with two perplexing questions that haunt us all.

TWO HAUNTING QUESTIONS ABOUT PAIN

Things aren't as they ought to be. There's a gap between *is* and *ought*, and many blame God for it. Christian author Udo Middelmann described how many view the world: "Reality is such a mess…. Someone in heaven must be behind all this, in the same way that there was always some evil ruler behind everything bad on earth."[1]

Not only is suffering real, but it's also everywhere. Like nuclear material poisoning the environment after a reactor meltdown, suffering contaminates every part of our lives no matter how hard we try to seal it off. Sometimes suffering results from human-caused evil. But evil is also present in nature. Each year disasters around the world disrupt the lives of tens of millions of people and kill tens of thousands more.[2]

The problem of pain is not theoretical to me. I've experienced the pain of bad choices made as a youth, pain of severe injury, pain of difficult circumstances, and pain of family breakdown. The list goes on. Through my divorce, the hurt I experienced felt so disabling that at times I didn't care whether I continued to live. Also, I've been a professor long enough to have been trusted to walk through pain with many of my students. I have cried with those who have lost a parent to disease or a tragic accident. I've felt my heart break as students described the abuse they have suffered. I've agonized with young adults who felt set aside in life because of addictions or a lack of clear direction.

As a divorced man who has walked through dark valleys, including a bout with depression, I've also found myself counseling ministry leaders facing crises. One told me, "I hate that you had to go through so much pain to be in a place where you can help me, but I'm grateful because I am tired and scared and don't know anyone else I can turn to." People don't confide in me because I'm a skilled counselor, believe me. Counseling utterly drains me. If I'm listening, it's because I'm at a loss for words. I'm not good at sitting still. But people in pain tend to trust those who have been there. And they all have the same two questions I've had: *Why* do I hurt? and *What* can I do to make it stop?

WHY DO I HURT?

Hurt is the pain we feel when our suffering seems meaningless. Austrian psychoanalyst Viktor Frankl, who survived a Nazi concentration camp, noticed that people bear up under pain as long as they see the meaning in it. If we understand why we're suffering, Frankl believed, it ceases to be suffering.[3]

I would agree. In college I broke my neck in a car accident. Most days since then I have woken with joint pain and headaches. My limited range of motion presents a challenge for physical activity, as further injury could lead to paralysis or death. (This takes much of the fun out of mountain biking, skiing, and other activities I love to be involved in.) Yet because my injury was part of a process of coming back to God, my pain was part of God's setting me on a new path. I still hurt—a lot sometimes—but it's not meaningless pain.

In my dream, when I was running down a lengthening hallway, I was convinced that the secret behind the door was not the end of the pain but the meaning behind it. If only I could reach the distant open door, I would recognize that what I see as broken threads have been, from the other side of the tapestry, woven into a breathtaking scene. Meanwhile, in the midst of pain, a second question pounds its way to the forefront.

WHAT CAN I DO TO STOP THE HURT?

We think that if we can figure out what caused our hurt, we can make it stop. Often, though, the search for answers takes us to a spiritually dark place where we see firsthand how evil has corroded what is good in this world.[4] Pain is the signal that evil is at work.

Many people have said to me, "I could never believe in a God who would allow people to suffer." It's a fair point: the Christian worldview ought to account for the presence of evil. But it's also fair to say that *every* worldview has the same problem. Are the explanations for evil provided by secularism, Marxism, postmodernism, new spirituality, and Islam any more satisfying?

IDENTIFYING THE LIES COUNTERFEIT WORLDVIEWS TELL ABOUT PAIN

Here's a summary description of what four of the five counterfeit worldviews says about why we hurt. Then we'll examine the explanation offered by new spirituality, as it takes the emotional side of the problem of pain most seriously and arrives at a very different kind of answer.

SECULARISM

The secular worldview says there is no spiritual realm, no ultimate good and evil. There is no higher cause or plan. As atheist Richard Dawkins has coldly stated, "In a universe of blind physical forces and genetic replication, some people are going to get hurt, other people are going to get lucky, and you won't find any rhyme or reason in it, nor any justice.... DNA neither knows nor cares. DNA just is. And we dance to its music."[5] Secularism suggests that we quit asking why and instead focus on managing the pain so we can regain control. The answer is, as the 1970s band Pink Floyd sarcastically sang, to become "comfortably numb."

MARXISM

The Marxist worldview says that all of reality is defined by revolutionary class struggle.[6] We experience pain because the rich have left us in misery by taking more than their fair share. The solution? Revolution.[7] Overthrow everything that keeps us down: the economy, the government, the family, even the church. Marx and his followers were particularly hard on the church because, they said, it keeps us down by intoxicating us with the "spiritual booze" of a promised—but mythical—heaven.[8] In a cruel irony, Marxism promises an end to pain, but in practice it is perhaps history's greatest source of human-caused suffering, extinguishing the lives of more than one hundred million people.[9]

POSTMODERNISM

To the postmodern worldview, there is no sure answer for why we endure pain and suffering. Worldviews that promise an earthly paradise always let us down, and any religion that promises a heavenly paradise will disappoint us even more. Suffering is absurd, the postmodern worldview says. Suffering will either make us laugh or cry, so we might as well laugh, like Sisyphus in the ancient Greek myth. He mocked the gods while carrying out his ridiculous sentence, which involved an eternity of pushing a boulder up a mountain, only to watch it roll back down again. Of Sisyphus, the absurdist philosopher Albert Camus (1913–1960) said, "There is no fate that cannot be surmounted by scorn."[10] In the same way, postmodernism says, we should embrace the absurd and quit expecting answers to questions that make no sense to begin with.

ISLAM

The Islamic worldview encourages people to stop asking questions about pain and suffering, but for a different reason. To Islam, God is in complete control. He is responsible for the evil that occurs and owes us no explanation.[11] To ask why evil exists is to ask the wrong question. We must simply obey.[12] "Such a life of obedience brings in peace of the heart and establishes real peace in the society at large," the revered Islamic scholar Khurshid Ahmad has written.[13] So, according to this worldview, what should we do about pain? Obey God and perhaps he will relent in his punishment.

SUFFERING IS AN ILLUSION: ISOLATING NEW SPIRITUALITY'S STEALTH ATTACK ON OUR HOPE FOR HEALING

It's hard to imagine four more diverse worldviews than the ones we've just examined. Yet they have two things in common. First, they place the blame for suffering "out there": as caused by nature, the rich, culture, or God. Second, they seek to eliminate pain and suffering by controlling its consequences: by managing its physical symptoms, overthrowing those thought to cause it, laughing at it, or acting according to strict rules to appease God. In the end, the proper response to evil is to blame others and numb ourselves to its effects.

When it comes to asking why we hurt, the new spirituality worldview says that everything that exists is one thing. If we are out of step with it, we'll hurt. As bestselling author Marilyn Ferguson explained, "Health and disease don't just happen to us. They are active processes issuing from inner harmony or disharmony, profoundly affected by our states of consciousness, our ability or inability to flow with experience."[14] Pain, disease, and listlessness all come from failing to attain this inner harmony.[15]

What can we do about the suffering we experience? New spirituality says that we should view it as an illusion and that the best response is to deny that it exists.[16] This view has a tradition extending back thousands of years. The *Bhagavad Gita*, a treasured stanza of Indian literature, has Lord Krishna responding to Arjuna's grief by saying,

> Although you mean well, Arjuna,
> Your sorrow is sheer delusion.
> Wise men do not grieve
> For the dead or for the living.[17]

We've fallen for a trick, Krishna argues. This world is not what is really real.[18]

Buddhism's approach to suffering runs along a parallel path.[19] In his first sermon, Buddha outlined several kinds of suffering, including birth, aging, sickness, death, sorrow, pain, grief, and despair. The cause of this suffering, he said, was attachment. Think of a monkey that reaches through a hole in a gourd and grasps a treat but gets trapped when it won't release the treat. Releasing attachment is the only way to be free. The end of suffering, Buddha said, is "the complete cessation of that very thirst, giving it up, renouncing it, emancipating oneself from it, detaching oneself from it."[20]

New spirituality borrows heavily from Hinduism and Buddhism. Stop being attached to the physical world. Let it go. Find harmony with the spiritual oneness of the universe and suffering will cease to have any meaning for you. This view faces criticism on many levels from other worldviews. One criticism hits deeper than the others. If we are suffering, new spirituality tells us, it's our own fault for not living in harmony with the universe. But people suffer accidents and all kinds of misery through no fault of their own. Think of a child affected by fetal alcohol syndrome, which causes developmental and physical disabilities, because her mom kept drinking during pregnancy. How can we say the child deserves this suffering?

What we believe about why we have pain will determine what we think will make it stop. Let's see what each worldview has to say about that.

COUNTERFEIT WORLDVIEWS LEAD TO COUNTERFEIT HEALING

Just as our senses are heightened when we are fighting off an infection, idea viruses loom larger when we are hurting. All we want is to make the aching and fever and sniffles stop.

Much of modern life is arranged to stop physical pain. Modern transportation eliminates the need to walk for miles to reach our destination. Well-designed buildings and roads and passenger vehicles make us safer so we don't cause ourselves injury. Fast food takes away the pain of hunger as well as the pain of waiting. Smartphones relax our anxiety over being out of touch or the embarrassment of not knowing the latest trends. We feel we are in control.

Although each of these innovations might have its downside, people almost universally approve of them. Beyond the helpfulness of modern conveniences, though, a secret battle rages over what pain and suffering mean and thus what we ought to do about them. The idea that is quickly gaining the upper hand, as we have seen, is that pain is essentially meaningless and that the best response is to numb it.

Pain is as much a philosophical issue as a medical one. Thoughts on pain can be found in the philosophy undergirding the Enlightenment-era rejection of traditional Christian thinking. In his book *Treatise on Man*, philosopher René Descartes theorized that the human body is like a machine and that pain was a physical sensation, not a spiritual one. This was seen as an improvement over Christianity, which came under fire in the Enlightenment because it supposedly *wanted* people to experience pain so they could suffer as Jesus did. Although the Bible does speak of wanting to know Christ and share in his suffering (see Phil. 3:10), this criticism doesn't tell the whole story. Not even close. In fact, as we will see in the next chapter, it has been Christians through history who took the lead in *alleviating* human suffering.

At the heart of the philosophical debate about pain and evil are these questions: Is ignoring the spiritual aspect of suffering a good idea? What if a great part of pain is spiritual, not physical?[21] If we're hurting because we feel afraid or unloved or purposeless, then numbing the pain cannot, in itself, make us feel better. Novocain can dull the throb of a toothache, but it can't make us smile when our life circumstances have us in tears.

Please understand, it is completely reasonable to try to alleviate physical pain. But if pain has a spiritual source, trying to alleviate it with physical remedies alone can cause more problems than it solves. One in every ten Americans over age twelve is addicted to illicit drugs and/or alcohol.[22] Another one in ten misuses prescription drugs.[23] Others overeat or look at pornography or devote too much time to technology and entertainment as a way of numbing their pain.

Even with all our remedies, we live in an age filled with spiritual pain. Although suicide among teens is a heartbreaking crisis, as a group, people in their forties and eighties—men in particular—are most likely to end their own lives.[24] This tells me that if we don't deal with our hurt in the right way, it becomes more unbearable through time.

Even those whose worldview tells them that pain is meaningless or an illusion still sense that things are not as they ought to be. C. S. Lewis concluded, "If the whole universe has no meaning, we should never have found out that it has no meaning: just as, if there were no light in the universe and therefore no creatures with eyes, we should never know it was dark. *Dark* would be a word without meaning."[25] Something's not right with the world. We all know it, even if our explanations can't explain it very well.

The one thing we cannot do is refuse to grapple with the problem of pain. The secret battle of ideas can't be avoided. It must be won. We need someone to step up and show us how to force pain to retreat. And indeed, someone has.

CHAPTER 6

WE SHALL OVERCOME

How Jesus Heals Our Hurts and Gives Us the Victory

DECLARATION: MY SUFFERING WILL BE OVERCOME. HURT WILL NOT WIN. INDEED, IT ALREADY HAS LOST.

Ernest Gordon's surroundings looked bleak. Men huddled, shivering with tropical diseases. Gordon had lost track of how many had died from starvation, disease, overwork, or execution. One man, Dusty, was hanged on a tree to die like Jesus. Others just lost hope and passed away in their sleep.

He thought back on the past few months. Gordon had been a proud Scottish warrior helping defend the British outpost of Singapore at the outbreak of World War II. Then the Japanese attacked. Now he found himself captive in the infamous Chungkai prison camp, where "the rhythm of death obsessed us with its beat."[1]

Then two remarkable things happened. First, word spread of a prisoner who, in the name of Jesus, offered his own food and stayed by the side of his bunkmate to nurse him back from the brink of death. His bunkmate survived, but he did not. Second, when a work detail was accused of stealing a shovel and its members were threatened with execution, one man stepped forward to "confess" to the theft to save the lives of the others. The enraged guard beat him, crushing his skull. A recount of the shovels showed none was missing.

What Gordon now saw defied explanation. In light of these sacrifices, the attitude in the camp quickly shifted from "me first" to "you first." Awakened from their self-pity, men changed one another's filthy bandages and even attended to the wounds of enemy soliders brought to the camp. The experience of death changed as prisoners stopped piling up bodies and instead elected chaplains to conduct funerals to honor the fallen. Life steadily regained meaning.

Restored to their humanity, the prisoners formed a library and taught courses in everything from math to philosophy to languages (nine of them). They staged plays. Having retrieved six violins from a relief shipment, they formed an orchestra and held concerts.

Camp conditions overall had not changed. Frightful diseases still claimed lives. Food was still scarce and nauseating. "Death was still with us—no doubt about that," wrote Gordon. "But we were slowly being freed from its destructive grip."[2] How these men were able to overcome the horrors of a POW camp offers deep insight into how a Christian worldview overcomes the idea viruses that multiply our suffering. Hurt will not win. Indeed, it has already lost. Here's how we know.

BE INFORMED: "NIKAO" AS THE CHRISTIAN WORLDVIEW'S RESPONSE TO PAIN AND SUFFERING

Pain and suffering baffle us. Con artists prey on the elderly. Children are killed at school. People commit horrible evil and escape punishment. Meanwhile, tornadoes, floods, fires, and other disasters wreak havoc on those we love.

Why does God allow this? Some religions try to put a happy face on the question, but a Christian worldview does not. The prophet Jeremiah asked, "Why does the way of the wicked prosper? Why do all who are treacherous thrive?" (Jer. 12:1). In Psalm 13:1, David cried out, "How long, O LORD? Will you forget me forever? How long will you hide your face from me?" Even the God-man Jesus Christ felt anguish over suffering. In the garden of Gethsemane, he said, "Father, if you are willing, remove this cup from me" (Luke 22:42).

One entire book of the Bible, Job, is devoted to spotlighting a good man's suffering. The book of Job might as well be titled *God, what the heck?* Terrible things happened to Job despite his faith in God. His children died. His business was destroyed. Painful disease racked his body. Job wondered, *Why is this happening?* God spoke to Job, but he didn't answer his burning question: *why?*

Still, Job never gave in, even when his wife advised him to curse God and die. Author Philip Yancey wrote, "Job clung to God's justice when he was the best example in history of God's apparent injustice. He did not seek the Giver because of his gifts; when all gifts were removed he still sought the Giver."[3]

In Yancey's statement are echoes of an ancient approach to suffering, one that replaces anger with humility, and self-pity with compassion.

As we saw in the previous chapter, counterfeit worldviews say that suffering is meaningless or an illusion and that our best responses are to blame others, numb the pain, or deny that suffering exists. But these views fall far short of the truth. Jesus's answer is much more robust. "In the world you will have tribulation," he said. "But take heart; I have overcome the world" (John 16:33).

Overcome. The word in Koine Greek is *nikao* (nick-AY-oh). As in Nike, the Greek goddess of victory (and, yep, shoes). *Nikao* doesn't just mean "winning"; it means "outlasting the enemy in a way that deprives it of its power to harm."

Hurt doesn't win; Jesus has overcome it. Hurt has been met on the battlefield and disarmed of its ability to rob us of what really matters. It's not that things are perfect. Pain and death persist. But as Gordon said about the Chungkai prison camp, we have been released from death's destructive grip. Jesus overcame; now we are overcomers.[4] This is possible because of four irresistibly powerful insights from the Bible about who God is, what has happened to the human race, and how God redeems us.

INSIGHT #1: GOD KNOWS EVERYTHING AND CAN DO AS HE CHOOSES

We humans are severely limited. I can hardly remember what I had for lunch yesterday and have no idea what will happen tomorrow.

God doesn't have this problem. He knows everything that is possible to know, past, present, and future.[5] He knows all truth. He believes no lies. He is perfect in knowledge. Romans 11:33 says, "Oh, the depth of the riches and wisdom and knowledge of God!" Being all-knowing, God is sovereign. He rules. He is in charge, and he will accomplish his purposes.

INSIGHT #2: GOD DOES NOT CHOOSE TO *DO* EVERYTHING

God can do whatever he chooses. Isaiah 46:11 says, "I have spoken, and I will bring it to pass; I have purposed, and I will do it." But God does not choose to do everything he is capable of doing. In this, the Christian worldview is quite different from the Muslim perspective. Islam teaches that God controls everything in the universe and that, as a result, free will is an illusion. The Bible, on the other hand, teaches that God created a world of laws in which humans can act meaningfully and that within that world, God gave us freedom of choice.[6] We are not puppets. There are no hidden strings manipulating us.

INSIGHT #3: HUMANS CHOOSE TO SIN

One of my children had a stuffed animal that, when squeezed, would say, "I love you. I love you." We all know that this isn't real love; it's just a programmed microchip. We can be truly loving only by being free to love or hate and then choosing love. When God created us as free creatures, he made it possible for us to choose to sin.[7] He created a world with stones in it, but people took up the stones and flung them at one another, causing pain.[8] The *potential* for evil is always there. We humans act on it and bring it to life.

INSIGHT #4: GOD CHOOSES TO REDEEM

The Christian worldview says that our sin need not doom us forever. There is a price to be paid, but Christ has paid it. We still suffer, but Christ has disarmed suffering of its ability to destroy us. Maybe this is why Peter encouraged his followers to rejoice in suffering. He had seen it disarmed in his own life. As a younger man, Peter had proclaimed his undying loyalty to Jesus. Jesus replied, "Truly, I tell you, this very night, before the rooster crows, you will deny me three times" (Matt. 26:34). Peter then did just as Jesus had foreseen. It wasn't the end of the story, though. After his resurrection, Jesus tenderly forgave Peter and recommissioned him for faithful service (see John 21:15–17). Why go through all that? Perhaps a fallen and redeemed Peter was better than an upright and self-righteous one.

The same is true for us. As we choose, God knows what will happen. When we arrive at the destination that is determined by the choices we make, we will see that God meets us there.[9]

These four insights (that God knows everything, that he does not choose to do everything, that humans choose to sin, and that God chooses to redeem) set the stage for a work of great magnificence: God's turning redemption from an *idea* into a *person* and doing it through suffering to end suffering.

HOW JESUS DEFEATS IDEA VIRUSES THAT KEEP US HURT

If you're looking for a thorough explanation for why God might allow suffering, there are lots of good books on the topic, such as *The Problem of Pain* by C. S. Lewis.[10] In *The Secret Battle of Ideas about God*, my goal is simply to show how we can be released from idea viruses that push us to blame others, numb our pain, or deny that pain exists. We do this by focusing on two key parts of the Christian worldview of suffering.

HOW JESUS IS THE ANSWER

God's answer to suffering is a life offered up in our place.[11] Jesus is with us. As poet Edward Shillito wrote in "Jesus of the Scars,"

> The other gods were strong;
> but Thou wast weak;
> They rode, but Thou didst stumble to a throne;
> But to our wounds only God's
> wounds can speak,
> And not a god has wounds, but Thou alone.[12]

Because of the cross, we have hope that God will conquer evil. In fact, the entire story of the Bible tells how he is doing just that. The cross sets the Christian worldview apart from every human-centered view. Theologian John Stott related his experience in Asian temples, standing before the statue of Buddha:

> I could never myself believe in God, if it were not for the cross.... In the real world of pain, how could one worship a God who was immune to it?... In imagination I have turned ... to that lonely, twisted, tortured figure on the cross, nails through hands and feet, back lacerated, limbs wrenched, brow bleeding from thorn-pricks, mouth dry and intolerably thirsty, plunged in Godforsaken darkness. That is the God for me![13]

This is a hugely important insight. The Christian worldview is not just about logical arguments; it's about Jesus personally dealing with evil and suffering. In addition to his suffering on the cross, Jesus's earthly ministry illustrates how he turned back the effects of sin. He healed people who were blind. He freed people tormented by demons. He raised people from the dead. Jesus didn't medicate suffering; he overcame it.

Knowing that God is with us in our suffering changes the whole arc of the world's story. Suffering isn't pointless. William Lane Craig is a respected philosopher who lives with a neuro-muscular disorder that slowly atrophies his muscles. Each day, he faces a choice to bear up under suffering and stay focused on knowing God more. In the midst of this, Craig wrote,

> If God does not exist, then we are locked without
> hope in a world filled with pointless and un-
> redeemed suffering. God is the final answer to
> the problem of suffering, for He redeems us from
> evil and takes us into the everlasting joy of an in-
> commensurable good: fellowship with Himself.[14]

Hope has arrived in the world, not as an idea but as a person. That's the first part of God's answer to evil and suffering. The second part of God's answer is you.

HOW YOU ARE THE ANSWER

Lots of people think the world will get worse no matter what we do, so why try? But if we take a larger view, we can see how the love of Christ patiently turns back suffering. According to researcher Scott Todd, extreme poverty has dropped in half over the past generation, from 52 percent of the world's population to 26 percent.[15] Since 1990, more than two and one-half billion people have gained access to improved water supplies.[16] Though tuberculosis remains a major killer, the death rate from it is down 40 percent in the last twenty or so years.[17] Polio cases have decreased by 99 percent since 1988.[18] Significant progress is being made in the fight against malaria as well.[19]

Christians from history would be encouraged by these trends, I believe. They thought that caring for the body was an important part of bearing God's image, so they tended to the sick during epidemics when everyone else, including physicians, fled. As documented by Cyprian, the bishop of Carthage, and Dionysius, bishop of Alexandria, during a Roman plague, Christians stayed behind and nursed the sick, often forfeiting their own lives in the process. The same thing happened during the Black Death in Europe (1346–53), when the mortality rate among the clergy was higher than that of the general population, as they risked their lives to care for the afflicted.

Throughout the Middle Ages, care of the seriously ill fell to Christian religious institutions. The Catholic Church was very influential, but so were sects such as the Moravian Brethren and Halle Pietists. Sir Thomas Percival (1740–1804), a Dissenter who studied theology prior to becoming a physician, helped create the field of occupational health and wrote an influential book on medical ethics. Today, hospitals founded by Catholics, Methodists, Baptists, Presbyterians, and others continue the tradition. Christian missions usually provide medical care as a matter of course.

Historically, the Christian view of suffering motivated Christians to take on the suffering of others. They accepted as literal Jesus's teaching about loving their neighbors (see Mark 12:31) and caring for the sick (see Matt. 25:34–40). They were convinced that the same Jesus who instructed them to care for bodily needs would care for their souls in the afterlife (see John 14:1–3). They did not fear death. Rather than blaming others, they worked for reform. Rather than merely numbing pain's effects, they ministered to deeper needs. Rather than denying that suffering is real, they developed a clear-eyed view of its causes and effects and worked toward solutions.

Blunting pain is not all there is to life, and we don't need to wait for a revolution to end suffering. Nor must we pretend that suffering has no meaning or is an illusion. Ours is not an unconcerned, frowning deity who cares little about our struggles. God is personally involved in turning back suffering, and we get to help.

INVEST IN YOURSELF AND OTHERS: FIVE THINGS YOU CAN DO RIGHT NOW TO FIND HEALING

A Christian worldview of suffering isn't just theoretical; it's something to be lived out every day. Here's how.

1. Dwell on God's presence. Acts 7:48 says that God does not dwell in houses made with human hands. He is here, now. Frank Laubach, a missionary who helped millions of poor people overcome illiteracy, decided as an experiment to make thinking about God a literal, minute-by-minute practice. He asked, *God, where are you in this moment? What do you want me to see and do?* It was the hardest thing he had ever done, but it made everything else easy.[20] Constantly remembering God's presence puts suffering in its place.

2. Serve. Galatians 6:2 says, "Bear one another's burdens." The famous psychiatrist Karl Menninger was asked what he thought someone should do if on the brink of a nervous breakdown. He replied, "Leave your house, find someone in need, and do something to help that person."[21]

3. Reject fate. Some people get discouraged and give up trying to change things for the better. We think, *What's the point?* Or we avoid helping by thinking, *They deserve it* or *I pay taxes—what more do you expect me to do?* When we don't see any hope, we ought to study Christians such as Amy Carmichael, one of the first to stand against sex trafficking (in the late 1800s). Carmichael showed how to display Christ's love by offering a warm heart rather than a cold shoulder. Thousands were restored to meaningful lives because of her work.[22]

4. Accept the love of others. When my marriage broke up, my first thought was *I don't have anyone to turn to.* It simply wasn't true. When I called out for help, people responded. This kind of help isn't like being in a hospital, though. It's more like being in church. In fact, it *is* being in church. The body of Christ functions when we live out our part faithfully and allow others to live out their parts in ways that serve us. If someone offers help, take it. If someone needs help, give it.

5. Look forward to a better day. This life is not all there is. As pastor Randy Alcorn has written, "One day, evil will end. Forever. Suffering and weeping are real and profound, but for God's children, they are temporary. Eternal joy is on its way."[23] Death is not a variable; it is a constant. The variable is how we live the days we are given. That's why the psalmist wrote, "Teach us to number our days that we may get a heart of wisdom" (Ps. 90:12). One of my friends, shortly before his death from cancer, said, "My prayer is that I will be conscious to the end so I can pray blessing over my family and friends." I'm sad at the loss of my friend but proud about how, in the midst of immense suffering, he stayed focused on finishing well.

ONE MORE THING

At the center of reality is Jesus and the cross. "Any discussion of how pain and suffering fit into God's scheme ultimately leads back to the cross," concluded Philip Yancey.[24] Jesus's cross was not one of defeat; it was one of victory. The apostle Paul wrote, "O death, where is your victory? O death, where is your sting?" (1 Cor. 15:55). The word *victory* here, as you might have guessed, is derived from *nikao*. Death has been overcome. It is because of this truth that we can each declare freedom from the idea viruses that unrelentingly prolong our anguish: *My suffering will be overcome. Hurt will not win. Indeed, it already has lost.*

It was through the power of the cross that Ernest Gordon and his fellow prisoners rose above their suffering. Is it possible to find this kind of meaning today in a busy and complex world where no one seems to care? In difficult times of my life, idea viruses in my mind and heart led me to ask, *If I were to disappear, would anyone even care?* What assurance do you and I have that our individual lives mean anything at all?

CHAPTER 7

DOES MY LIFE HAVE MEANING?

How Idea Viruses Strip Us of Direction and Leave Us Aimless

His nickname was the Little Pastor. According to his sister, Elizabeth, "He could recite biblical texts and hymns with such feeling that he almost made one cry."[1] As a young man, he wrote of his commitment to Christ, "I have firmly resolved within me to dedicate myself forever to His service. May the dear Lord give me strength and power to carry out my intentions and protect me on my life's way."[2]

But by age seventeen, the young man started to change. He wrote, "If we could examine Christian doctrine and Church history with a free, unconstrained eye, we would be compelled to arrive at many conclusions which contradict generally accepted ideas."[3]

Before long, the young man began thinking of "gods" as human creations. Jesus was a good role model, he surmised, but Christianity's influence had come to an end. People just didn't believe any longer. In a now-famous passage, he wrote as a madman confronting his fellow citizens about God's death:

> Whither is God?... I will tell you. *We have killed him*—you and I. All of us are his murderers.... Is not night continually closing in on us? Do we not need to light lanterns in the morning? Do we hear nothing as yet of the noise of the gravediggers who are burying God? Do we smell nothing as yet of the divine decomposition? Gods, too, decompose. God is dead. God remains dead. And we have killed him.[4]

Only the widespread belief in God had kept God alive, according to this man. People had stopped believing, so God was dead. We had murdered him with our minds.

Plagued by mental illness, the man descended into madness. His name was Friedrich Nietzsche (1844–1900). Regarded as a brilliant philosopher, Nietzsche is most admired not because he was an atheist—lots of philosophers condemn belief in God—but because he grappled honestly with the dark shadows his philosophy cast.

Nietzsche wrote during a time of extraordinary scientific and economic achievement. People used to pray to God to keep from getting sick and to make their crops grow and to give them daily bread. Now it seemed that humans could accomplish anything. Who needs God?

Yet Nietzsche saw downstream, where this current of thought would lead. Belief in God had been Western civilization's guiding hand in the areas of morality and meaning. Who would take God's place? We humans would, Nietzsche thought. We'll be brave and exert our "will to power." We'll become *Übermensch*, German for "superman." This idea led to unthinkable consequences. Decades after Nietzsche's death, his idea of the superman became the central guiding force of a political movement called National Socialism, led by Adolf Hitler.[5] The twentieth century already had been catastrophic, with war and disease killing millions. When it couldn't possibly get any worse, it got worse.

Like Nietzsche, each of us is swept up in a search for meaning. It's part of being human. But it also makes us vulnerable to idea viruses spread by those who have anointed themselves as "supermen" to remake the world. The struggle to find meaning opens up a whole new front in the secret battle of ideas.

Meanwhile, our hearts cry out with deep questions: Does my life count for anything? Are my hopes and dreams pointless? Does my existence on this planet matter? We need to know whether today's dominant worldviews meet these deep needs or whether they are idea viruses that leave us with even greater uncertainty.

IDENTIFYING THE LIES COUNTERFEIT WORLDVIEWS TELL ABOUT MEANING

Without a strong sense of purpose, people become vulnerable to dangerous ideas. The idea virus of Nazism targeted aimless people who felt oppressed and beset by unseen enemies. A third of German voters selected Hitler outright in the election of 1932. Reasserting their national will, they believed, would give them the meaning they sought. Aimlessness opened a crack into which one of history's worst idea viruses inserted itself, inflicting disaster on the world.

Once again, aimlessness reigns. Among today's young adults, only 40 percent strongly agree there is an ultimate purpose in life.[6] Stanford University professor William Damon has said that only about one in five young people ages twelve to twenty-two say they know where they want to go in life, what they want to accomplish, and why.[7]

Each of the worldviews we're considering promises to confront aimlessness by making big changes in the world. Our lives will have meaning, these worldviews say, if we become part of their sweeping agenda. But most people I know aren't looking for one more thing to sign up for. We want more of an everyday meaning that helps us become better family members and neighbors, find joy in our work, experience the blessings of love and friendship, and make wise decisions about how to live together in harmony.

Even those who embrace the worldviews we've studied say they want this, so it seems unfair to summarize in just a few words what each worldview says about life's meaning. Still, each worldview needs to be considered based on where its assumptions lead, not based on its rhetoric. Let's look at each worldview briefly and then explore the postmodern worldview more fully, as it attracts many who wonder whether meaning even exists.

SECULARISM

Secularism says there is no ultimate meaning—that the material world is all there is. Every problem is a material problem and therefore can be addressed by only a material solution. In the absence of ultimate meaning, people gain value from their relationships and their environment. Our aimlessness, then, comes from defective relationships and an unsupportive environment. We are the product of our society. Society constrains us—and society must set us free.[8]

But who exactly makes up the society responsible for giving us the meaning we seek? Because only the material world exists, those who believe in anything beyond what we experience with our five senses are either defective or delusional. They can't help us. Science and reason are our only hope, so smart people need to be in charge. Members of one secularist group vying for influence in society call themselves Brights, implying that those who disagree are dull.[9] Somehow, secularists have come to believe that because their "religion switch" is turned off, they're more qualified to lead.

But if nature can't provide meaning and if the material world is all there is, even the brightest of the Brights will be at a loss to help people discover a compelling reason to live other than just avoiding death.

MARXISM

Marxists encourage people to rise up in revolution against outside forces that keep them from living meaningful lives. These outside forces include government, the economy, the family, and the church. Overthrowing such forces would bring meaning to people's lives. The Soviets spoke often of the "new man" who would emerge from the pursuit of communism. Russian physiologist Ivan Pavlov, the guy who famously conducted research on dogs, told his laboratory assistants, "We may use all of the experimental material for the investigation of the human being, striving to perfect the human race of the future."[10]

Unfortunately, the "new man" ideal didn't restore meaning, as the Russian revolutionaries hoped it would. Several years ago, the movie *Enemy at the Gates* captured Marxism's failure to create a society in which all wealth was redistributed and everyone was equal. As the ace Russian sniper Vassili waited patiently for his target, his friend Danilov said,

> I've been such a fool, Vassili. Man will always be man. There is no new man. We tried so hard to create a society that was equal, where there'd be nothing to envy your neighbor. But there's always something to envy. A smile, a friendship, something you don't have and want to appropriate. In this world, even a Soviet one, there will always be rich and poor—rich in gifts, poor in gifts; rich in love, poor in love.[11]

Rather than ending pent-up frustration and envy, Marxism unleashed it. Nations fell. For tens of millions of people, the

Marxist worldview did not end their search for meaning. It ended their very lives.

NEW SPIRITUALITY

Eckhart Tolle is one of the bestselling authors of our time. His books and multiple appearances on widely viewed programs such as *The Oprah Winfrey Show* have turned him into a spiritual phenomenon. A small, unassuming man, Tolle startles his audience by spending the first several minutes of his presentation looking around the room, not saying a word. He calls this "practicing presence." By this he means contemplating his oneness with the audience and ridding himself of ego. To Tolle, the central problem with humanity is thinking we are separate individuals. Instead, we are—all together—one collective soul. The sooner we recognize this, the sooner we will find meaning in life.[12]

Although some worldviews say we gain meaning by focusing on ourselves, the new spirituality worldview leads followers in the opposite direction. Based on the Buddhist tradition, it denies the self altogether. The idea of the "soul or self," said the Dalai Lama, the Buddhist spiritual leader of Tibet, is "the source of all our misery."[13] Only when we rid ourselves of ego and become one with the universe can we be set free from meaninglessness. New-spiritualist author Ken Carey said, "Everyone anywhere who tunes into the Higher Self becomes part of the transformation. Their lives then become orchestrated from other realms."[14] All you have to do is give up your individual identity.

ISLAM

Islam says meaning comes through submission to God. The Quran states, "Those who believe, and whose hearts find satisfaction in the remembrance of Allah:... For those who believe and work righteousness, is (every) blessedness, and a beautiful place of (final) return" (13:28–29).[15] Muslims engage in daily prayer and other rituals that they believe will conquer faithlessness and build a global community of people who are obedient to Allah.

The path to meaning comes from jihad, which is the command to Muslims to master their rebelliousness and restore all people, by force if necessary, to their original state of being Muslim. Many Muslims believe that jihad might properly involve war against nonbelievers. The Quran seems to guarantee eternal reward to those who die in this effort.[16]

Unfortunately, many Muslim converts fall into the hands of people eager to radicalize them, such as Anwar al-Awlaki, born in Las Cruces, New Mexico, who was behind the online magazine *Inspire*. It's an online terrorist magazine whose first issue included an article titled "Make a Bomb in the Kitchen of Your Mom."[17] Dzhokhar and Tamerlan Tsarnaev built and detonated such a bomb at the 2013 Boston Marathon, killing three people and injuring hundreds of others. Similar bombs were planted, and one exploded, in an attack in New York City in 2016.

For most Muslims, submitting to God means having families, working hard, and practicing religious disciplines. For some, though, it means making one's mark by committing violent acts.

Only a tiny percentage of Muslims seem willing to take this step. The problem, though, is that it's hard to predict who will act this way and when.

Secularism, Marxism, new spirituality, and Islam are very different worldviews. They differ vastly in what they think is wrong with the world and what ought to be done about it. Yet one worldview, postmodernism, lumps these worldviews together and criticizes them because of one thing they have in common: they all believe their story of the world is the true one.

NO "THERE" THERE: ISOLATING A POSTMODERN WORLDVIEW OF MEANING

We're all distracted. From our first waking moment to our last conscious thought each day, we're hammered with information. Every passing minute, 204,166,667 email messages are sent, YouTube users upload forty-eight hours' worth of new video, Twitter users send more than 100,000 tweets, and Instagram users share 3,600 new photos.[18] By the time you read this, the numbers will be even higher.

In our distracted state, we tend to pick up lots of little stories—thirty-minute television programs, three-minute songs, thirty-second commercials, billboard slogans, bumper-sticker mottoes, and social-media memes—without ever grasping the bigger story and what it means for our lives. We're left with thousands of fragmented plot points and no overarching narrative holding them together.

Idea viruses hitch a ride in these messages. Yet the very way they're transmitted forms an idea virus as well: with lots of little stories and no overarching story, it's easy to conclude that there *is* no overarching story. That's the essential claim of the postmodern worldview. There are no big stories about life that are really true. There's no "there" there. Personal experience is our only source of meaning.

For postmodernist Michel Foucault, what Nietzsche said about the meaninglessness of God also applies to us. Humanity itself no longer has meaning: "It is not so much the absence or the death of God that is affirmed as the end of man.... New gods, the same gods, are already swelling the future Ocean; man will disappear."[19] All we can do in response to this is stop accepting people's labels, stop letting them push us to the margins, and stop letting them persuade us of "objective" standards of truth.[20]

The postmodern worldview says that there is no ultimate meaning in life and that we ought to be suspicious of those who say there is.[21] Often you'll hear those with this worldview say "I define myself" and "You can't tell me what to do" and "It may be true for you but not for me." Other worldviews—not just the Christian worldview—challenge postmodernism's claim. Measuring yourself by yourself is like navigating through the wilderness by throwing away your compass and pretending you *are* magnetic north. Not only would you be forever lost, but you'd also mislead everyone looking to you for guidance.

Indeed, the very idea that there is such a thing as an "I" who ought to search for meaning is seen as absurd.[22] To use postmodern jargon, we humans are just ever-evolving, highly sexual, social animals with multiple subjective interests crying out for recognition and acceptance.[23] Postmodernism says we are like onions, with layer after layer of culture. When we're done peeling, nothing remains. We have no core. Meaning is an illusion.

COUNTERFEIT WORLDVIEWS LEAD TO COUNTERFEIT MEANING

So to the secular worldview, we gain meaning only through our relationships and the environment. The Marxist worldview says we gain meaning through revolution. The new spirituality worldview says we gain meaning by ridding ourselves of ego. The Islamic worldview says we gain meaning through submission to God. The postmodern worldview says there is no meaning "out there" to be gained in the first place.

The postmodern embrace of Nietzsche's idea that there are no fixed standards for truth is alarming. In the twentieth century, this idea virus created a vacuum that groups such as the Nazis filled.[24] Indeed, they justified their brutality with Nietzsche's writings. The "strong men, the masters," according to Nietzsche, were not bound by any moral code. They could commit murder, arson, rape, and torture with "joy in their hearts."[25]

In the end, though, the Nazis didn't need Nietzsche's stamp of approval. They just summoned his ghost and channeled it into the spirit of the age. What began as an idea virus plaguing the search for meaning spread into a pandemic in Europe and beyond,

annihilating Jews, Poles, gypsies, homosexuals, people with disabilities, and others who did not qualify to be part of the Nazis'
master race. It took a world war to stop them.

In our aimlessness, we are wide open to destructive idea
viruses. If we each had a strong sense of purpose in life, we might
be able to resist them. But to other worldviews, there's always
something holding us back from gaining meaning, whether it is
religion, capitalism, the lack of global consciousness, rebellion
against Allah, or even the search for truth itself. Nothing will
change until everything changes.

So do our lives have any meaning? It seems we're right back
where we started, or perhaps even worse off than before. Should
we just abandon our search altogether, or is there a higher purpose
that can make our lives meaningful? Personally, I hold out hope
because of a startling lesson I learned from a sled dog in the frigid
wilderness near Fairbanks, Alaska.

CHAPTER 8

HEARING THE CALL

How Jesus Restores Meaning to Our Lives

DECLARATION: I HAVE AN INCREDIBLE CALLING. MY LIFE HAS MEANING. I BEAR GOD'S IMAGE.

I answered the phone on a Thursday morning. A voice asked, "Would you consider coming to Alaska to speak? We'll pay your fee and cover your airfare, hotel, and meals. And we'll send you on a three-day tour."

It was clearly the Lord's will for me to go to Alaska.

I arrived in Anchorage during the Iditarod, the legendary sled-dog race. This contest of more than a thousand miles memorializes the 1925 relay in which a lead dog named Balto guided Gunnar Kaasen through eighty-mile-per-hour winds to deliver lifesaving serum to the people of diphtheria-ravaged Nome.

Caught up in the enchantment surrounding this epic event, I visited the Iditarod headquarters to follow the race's progress and chat with past champions. Meanwhile, an idea grew in my mind. If I could find an experienced musher, I might be able to try this sport out for myself. As it turned out, a sled-dog hobbyist named William agreed to show me the wonders of dog-powered travel.

In the yard of his neatly organized but primitive cabin near Fairbanks, William cared for twenty-five enthusiastic sled dogs. For our adventure, William patiently harnessed eight of them to a sled. The remaining dogs yelped and whined, but one dog seemed determined to break free and join us. She strained against her leash, lunged, and flipped over. Again and again she tried to get William's attention.

Awed by her resolve, I said, "William, I think that dog would like to go with us." William glanced over his shoulder and said softly, "She can't go. She's injured."

Observing her wild antics, I could easily see how this dog might injure herself. Recklessly committed, she soon broke free and chased after us. William chuckled and rigged a harness for her, continuing without a word.

As we glided along the snowy trail, William issued soft commands with a Zen-like calmness. The dogs obeyed. Returning to base some three hours later, I said, "William, you practically whispered your commands and the dogs followed them. How did you do that?"

His answer carved a path in my heart that I now realize leads to victory in the secret battle of ideas about life's meaning. You and I have incredible callings that release us from idea viruses that would leave us aimless. Here's how we can know.

BE INFORMED: "KALEO" AS THE CHRISTIAN WORLDVIEW RESPONSE TO AIMLESSNESS

When philosophers wonder about meaning, they seek answers to three questions: What is real? How can we know? And finally, how should we live? With idea viruses running rampant, it's hard to find answers. Few people are confident of their life's purpose. This is not just a disoriented generation; it's a generation without a destination.

My own search for clarity helps explain why William's answer to my question was so life changing. How did he get an entire team of energetic animals to respond to his quiet, gentle guidance? "These dogs were *made* for this," he explained. "They *live* for this. And when you're doing what you're designed to do, your master can guide you with a whisper."

The dogs responded because William was working with their nature, not against it. By harnessing them to run, William was in fact unleashing them. They were born to run. To employ a phrase at which my English teacher would cringe, running is something those dogs could not *not* do. I've since learned two insights about how these dogs' inbred confidence applies to each one of us.

INSIGHT #1: THERE IS SOMETHING MORE TO LIFE

As William spoke, I wondered, *What is it that I cannot* not *do?* I thought back on the crisis of meaning I suffered early in my college career. Law school seemed to fit naturally into my trajectory. After a few prelaw classes left me unmoved, though, I mentioned to a fraternity brother that I was switching majors. Dumbfounded, he asked, "Why would you turn your back on success?"

"I've wondered the same thing," I admitted. "But I'm not like you. You love studying law. Personally, I would rather be homeless than have to practice law for the rest of my life."

"So what are you going to major in?"

"Communications."

"Well," he remarked dryly, "that's a good major for an aspiring homeless person."

Many saw communications as a brainless course of study with no job prospects. But I *loved* classes in communications. They gave me energy and brought me to life. Sure, I wanted a job. After all, I like food and shelter as much as the next person. But I wanted something more.

At the time I met William and his sled dogs, I had just completed graduate school and gotten a good job as a professor. I had a beautiful wife and young son. We lived in a quaint home with a long front porch. My dreams were coming true. Still, I couldn't shake the question Is this all there is? Looking back, I can see that idea viruses were prompting me to orient my search for meaning around money, power, reputation, and adventure. I risked turning into someone I didn't want to be.

Most people sense that life is something more than they've experienced in the past. Each worldview must account for this. Some counterfeit worldviews convince us that a search for meaning is fruitless because the only meaning is that which we make for ourselves. Others persuade us that a glorious death through revolution or jihad will bring us a promised paradise. "We love death more than you love life," read a warning note found at the scene of a would-be terrorist bombing in London.[1]

Starting the day I met William and the sled dogs, I began discovering that a Christian worldview rises above these extremes. At the intersection of confusion and death, Jesus pointed in an entirely new direction. "The thief comes only to steal and kill and destroy," he said. "I came that they may have life and have it abundantly" (John 10:10). Like sled dogs, we can live meaningfully. Job said, "Ask the beasts, and they will teach you" (Job 12:7). The sled dogs taught me a memorable lesson.

Yet although I found myself inspired to listen to the Master's whisper, as William had phrased it, I wondered, *How do I make this insight a practical one?* Meaning comes instinctively to animals, but we humans seem to live in a fog. Many wander into the fog and don't even realize they are lost. Others, seeing the fog, turn back, giving up on the possibility of finding meaning. Still others, braving the fog, lose their bearings and panic. Only a few navigate successfully toward clarity. The Bible's explanation for why these few make it through the fog is both simple and overwhelming: they hear a voice calling them, and they follow it. You and I can do the same.

INSIGHT #2: WE ARE CALLED

The Christian worldview says reality opens up to those who will see Christ in all and over all. Abraham Kuyper, theologian and onetime prime minister of the Netherlands, said, "There is not one square inch of the entire creation about which Jesus Christ does not cry out, 'This is mine! This belongs to me!'"[2] All authority belongs to Jesus (see Matt. 28:18).

Not only that, but we are also made for great things. Psalm 139:13–14 says,

> You formed my inward parts;
> > you knitted me together in my mother's
> > womb.
> I praise you, for I am fearfully and wonderfully
> > made.
> Wonderful are your works;
> > my soul knows it very well.

God designed us to be like him, to bear the *imago Dei*, the "image of God." In the time of the Bible's writing, kings often displayed their authority by erecting statues of themselves. God didn't make statues; instead, he formed living, breathing humans to display his glory.

As image bearers, we don't possess God's glory; rather, we reflect it. When we move in the direction God has for us, we reflect his glory more brightly, like polished mirrors. When we go our own way, it's as if we're trying to display our own glory. It always comes across as silly and cheap, like settling for shiny Mardi Gras beads instead of the brilliant splendor of the Hope Diamond. As Jeremiah 2:11 says, "My people have changed their glory for that which does not profit."

God's image is our glory; reflecting his purposes is the key to our own purposes. The Bible refers to this as a calling. Romans 8:28 says, "We know that for those who love God all things work together for good, for those who are called according to his purpose." The word *call* is related to the Greek word *kaleo*. It means "to summon." Our Creator and Redeemer summons us.

Sometimes the ancient word *kaleo* is translated "vocation." It's an accurate translation, but it can be distracting because to us, *vocation* means "job." A calling is much more than a job. Jobs give us work; a calling gives us meaning. When sled dogs pull a musher across frozen tracks in Alaska, they're not just working; they are living out their calling.

Overcome by idea viruses, though, we end up searching for meaning in our environment (secularism), our ability to overthrow the systems that keep us down (Marxism), our cynicism that calls into question the existence of meaning (postmodernism), our skill at becoming one with the universe (new spirituality), or our determination to strictly follow Allah's law (Islam). The Christian worldview, however, says that the One who knows all things is calling out to us personally, healing us from idea viruses and restoring meaning in our lives.

HOW JESUS'S CALL DEFEATS THE IDEA VIRUS OF AIMLESSNESS

Clarence Darrow, the defense attorney in the historic *Scopes* trial, grumbled, "The purpose of man is like the purpose of the pollywog—to wiggle along as far as he can without dying; or, to hang to life until death takes him."[3] I understand the despair; often life has squashed my dreams. As the vocal group Twenty One Pilots sang,

> [We] used to dream of outer space,
> But now they're laughing at our face, saying,
> "Wake up, you need to make money."[4]

There's nothing wrong with making money, of course. Yet we wonder if there is more to life. The Christian worldview says there is much more value to work than merely making money. In Genesis 2, before the fall, God commanded Adam to work and keep the garden of Eden—literally, to serve it and watch over it. The Hebrew word for work, *abad*, means "to serve." Interestingly, it is one of the words used for worship.[5] Work is worship, and worship is work. Apparently, for Adam, going into the garden to work was a worshipful experience: work drew him closer to God. It was awesome—for a while, anyway.

After the fall, work became drudgery. We read in Genesis 3:17 that God told Adam, "Cursed is the ground because of you; in pain you shall eat of it all the days of your life." In Ecclesiastes 2:22, Solomon moaned, "What has a man from all the toil and striving of heart with which he toils beneath the sun?" We work for years on a project, only to have it canceled because of budget cuts. We grow a crop and then a drought destroys it. The students we teach don't rise to their potential.

Sin turned work into drudgery. In the Bible, the Hebrew and Greek words used for sin have to do with losing our way. "God saw the earth, and behold, it was corrupt, for all flesh had corrupted their way on the earth" (Gen. 6:12). There is a way that leads to life, the Bible affirms, but most have chosen the way of death. That's humanity's predicament: we have lost our way. Our very purpose for living seems compromised; our daily activities seem pointless.

Through Christ, we can regain the purpose we lost in the fall. On a wooden cross fashioned for humiliation and ugliness, a hardworking carpenter-God rescues us and fashions for us a holy calling of purpose and grace (see 2 Tim. 1:9). This calling leads us to meaning in at least three ways:

1. **Calling secures our identity.** A calling from God harmonizes who we are with what we ought to do. It completes our identities: the gifts and convictions that make up who we are.[6]

2. **Calling wards off idea viruses.** Calling is like an immune system, warding off the idea viruses that, like the sniffle and cough of a cold, throw us off track and make us miserable.

3. **Calling makes every area of our lives meaningful.** Calling infuses everyday life with great purpose. God is with us in our cubicles, in our laundry rooms, and in line at the grocery store.

Calling transforms drudgery. A number of years ago, a man mentioned to me that he delivers packages for a living. "Where is the meaning in it?" he asked. I found myself wishing this man could meet Buddy, the funny and cheerful UPS man who for years delivered packages to our house. One time, members of my family wrote, "Hi, Buddy!" on the driveway using sidewalk chalk. Later, a reply appeared on the pavement: "UPS rocks." Buddy didn't just have a job; he had a calling. Jesus rode along with Buddy every day.

Still, many turn away from God's call. The physician Luke shared Jesus's parable of calling people to a great banquet. The honored guests refused to come, distracted by their responsibilities. They missed the one thing that would have given meaning to the rest of their lives. The call came, and they couldn't—or wouldn't—hear it (see Luke 14:16–24). How can we not be like them?

INVEST IN YOURSELF AND OTHERS: FOUR THINGS YOU CAN DO RIGHT NOW TO HEAR JESUS'S CALL

When I tell the story about the sled dogs, people tell me they want to hear God's call but don't know how to go about doing so. I find myself explaining it in different ways, but these four things are at the heart of it:

1. Tune in to God's revelation in creation. Look for ways God expresses his call. David, a powerful king, humbly wrote,

When I look at your heavens, the work of your
fingers,
the moon and the stars, which you have set
in place,
what is man that you are mindful of him,
and the son of man that you care for him?
(Ps. 8:3–4)

In this instance, David surrendered to God's voice as expressed in the beauty of creation. Beauty, Harvard professor Elaine Scarry said, helps us realize that not only are we not the center of the universe, but we aren't even the center of our own world.[7] Every day, make it a point to look for God's call in creation's beauty—in trees, stars, the sunset, living creatures—and give praise.

2. Start discovering your unique design. Each person possesses unique gifts. Based on detailed interviews with more than one hundred thousand people, author and speaker Arthur F. Miller showed that each person is motivated to achieve certain outcomes and fulfill specific purposes, as if pulled by a magnet.[8] He called these purposes "motivated abilities."

Here's an example. My three siblings are all musicians but with very different motivated abilities. My sister, a piano teacher, finds delight in the joy of students as they learn to play music rather than just listen to it. One of my brothers, a worship leader, finds it satisfying when music draws people closer to God. My other brother, an orchestra conductor, loves organizing talented people to perform beautiful and complicated works of music.

God gave you your motivated abilities, and no one can take them away from you. You can discover them by asking questions such as the following:

- What are some of the things that return energy to me and make me feel more alive?
- What do I long for?
- What makes me tick?
- What captivates my imagination?

No two people answer these questions alike, even if their jobs are similar. Each person's design is unique.

3. Rethink the value of work. God intends for us to find meaning in the things we do every day. Meaning grows as we build on our experiences. As a young conductor, my brother Tim was mentored by the great Lorin Maazel, a genius who spoke seven languages and conducted symphonies from memory. Tim once asked Maestro Maazel his secret. Maazel said, "Be the best conductor you can be on day one. Then on day two, improve. Do that every day for your whole life and you'll be a great conductor." As Tim was absorbing this advice, Maazel added, "By the way, *today* is day one."

If you want to be a more effective public speaker, for example, you have to say yes to as many opportunities as possible, starting now. The same holds true if you want to be better at reading people or if you want to improve at discerning financial trends. Practice is not limited to rote repetition. It means *improving* in some way with every step taken. There are no shortcuts. World-renowned pianist Van Cliburn practiced six hours a day even after he gained international renown.[9] Progressing is not as hard as you think. Studies have shown that people experience substantial improvement in their skills with an investment of as little as two hundred hours. That's less than one hour a day for a year. Daily improvement is the route to success. The Japanese call it *kaizen*: daily change for the better.

4. Find activities that create flow. Born in 1934 to a Hungarian family, Mihály Csíkszentmihályi (pronounced Cheek-SENT-me-high) is a psychology professor whose research has led to many breakthroughs in productivity and satisfaction in people's lives. In one study, published in 1984, Csíkszentmihályi tracked seventy-five teenagers, asking them at random points throughout the day to record what they were doing and their level of happiness at that moment.[10] Though Csíkszentmihályi does not claim to be a believer, his discoveries nonetheless bear out much of what the Christian worldview says about work and purpose.

Csíkszentmihályi found that when teenagers channeled their energy toward meaningful tasks, they developed a higher level of satisfaction, a state that he termed *flow*.[11] Flow occurs when people engage in challenging tasks with clear goals and immediate feedback. Those experiencing flow forget about themselves and lose track of time.[12] Conversely, participants in the study reported the lowest levels of flow when they were just passing time, for example, by watching television.[13] To get flow, one has to be *doing* something.

Flow weaves together our unique design and the value of work. We find flow when we work hard at discovering that which is deeply compelling to us. Winston Churchill, Great Britain's inspirational leader during World War II, was an avid landscape painter. It helped him relieve stress and restore creativity. "A change is as good as a rest," Churchill said.

Tuning in to creation, discovering our unique designs, working hard, and finding flow are some of the ways the Christ-focused worldview imparts meaning in a world so many find meaningless.

ONE MORE THING

With the Christian worldview, meaning comes through callings based on who God made us to be. Each one of us can make this declaration of freedom: *I have an incredible calling. My life has meaning. I bear God's image.*

We are intricately created in the image of a thoughtful, whimsical, hardworking, proactive, "can-do" deity. It's through his call—not through control or revolution or cynicism or becoming one with the universe or blind obedience—that God shows us the way to meaning. We can ignore idea viruses that insist "My life isn't special" or "It's just a job" or "What I do just doesn't matter in the long run." Instead, like sled dogs, we can be guided by the whispered voice of the Master.

And yet the pursuit of meaning runs into trouble when lots of people who are seeking personal meaning begin colliding with one another. We wonder, *Why can't we all get along?* Sometimes the conflicts we face are merely irritating. Sometimes they're alarming. News reports about terrorist attacks and rogue armies and beheadings make peace seem further away than it ever has been before.

To see if today's popular worldviews have any answers, we need to get right to the heart of one of today's most perplexing conflicts. It started with a bombing that took place decades ago, targeting a man you've probably never heard of, in a town whose name is unfamiliar, in a country most people could never find on a map. And yet it unleashed an idea virus with tragic consequences that calls into question everything we thought we knew about peace.

CHAPTER 9

WHY CAN'T WE JUST GET ALONG?

How Idea Viruses Destroy the Peace We Crave

Peshawar, Pakistan. The bomb detonated just as a car passed over the culvert. The vehicle was blown in two, and its three occupants died instantly. One of the bodies was found intact, a man who looked as if he were sleeping, except for a trickle of blood coming from his mouth.[1] If the curious bystanders had known the chaos this man's death would unleash, they would have recoiled in fear. The explosion's victims included Abdullah Yusuf Azzam and two of his sons. Azzam's name may not be familiar, but you've certainly heard of Al-Qaeda, the terrorist organization he founded.

Upon receiving confirmation of Azzam's death, a wealthy young Saudi allowed himself a grim smile.[2] Once Azzam's protégé, the Saudi reportedly had begun to suspect the older man of the unforgivable sin of collaborating with America. The young man's name was Osama bin Laden. With his rise, a new deadly virus slipped noiselessly into humanity's bloodstream. Over the coming decades, it would break out in horrifying attacks in New York City, London, Paris, Brussels, Istanbul, Mumbai, Boston, and other cities around the world.

But Al-Qaeda didn't limit its attacks to the use of bombs and guns; it also attacked with ideas, recruiting disillusioned Westerners into its ranks. Now the Al-Qaeda offshoot, ISIS, draws half its fighters from foreign countries, including Western nations such as Britain, France, Germany, and the United States.[3]

Terrorism is beginning to seem like the new normal, and along with it comes the constant hum of worry, uncertainty, and fear. Unfortunately, this is the story of nearly all of human history. Journalist and Presbyterian minister Chris Hedges noted that "of the past 3,400 years, humans have been entirely at peace for 268 of them, or just 8 percent of recorded history."[4]

Below the surface of global turmoil is a secret battle of ideas competing for our allegiance. It's not just a battle for territory; it's also a battle for our hearts. "Death and life are in the power of the tongue," says Proverbs 18:21. With every harsh word, angry social-media meme, or whispered criticism of another bearer of God's image, we bring death to relationships. We also die a little ourselves.

With the escalation of this war, is our way of life dying as well? It's clear that we have trouble getting along with one another. The world longs for answers. The fate of nations lies in the balance. Our relationships with coworkers, family members, and neighbors are at stake. Unless we can figure out where conflict comes from and unflinchingly examine what today's dominant worldviews propose to do about it, with each passing day, we risk moving further away from peace and closer to constant conflict.

CONFLICT IS "OUT THERE," BUT IT'S ALSO "IN HERE"

The word *conflict* comes from the Latin for "strike together." Every conflict starts as an idea virus that then spreads out of control. Adolf Hitler took the idea virus of racial purity and turned Germany into a death factory. A similar thing happened as Joseph Stalin took the idea virus of Communist revolution and liquidated millions by shooting, starvation, and slave labor.

Yet the Nazi and Communist crimes took place in view of millions of people who could have stepped in but instead chose to remain uninvolved. Why didn't they do something? The uncomfortable answer to that question is the key to grasping how conflict does its destructive work. Nazi and Communist leaders got away with mass murder because citizens either didn't see where those ideas would lead or hesitated to step in before threats and intimidation from secret police and their informers made it impossible.

Conflict arises when we view ourselves in ways that diminish the value of others. It is human nature to assert our own purity by comparing ourselves with those whose deeds are demonstrably worse: *I am not as bad as "those people," so therefore I am good.* From there, it's a short step to *The world would be better off without "them."* A spirit of self-righteousness precedes every act of great evil.

Terrorist groups, for example, define their identity in a way that diminishes the value of others: *We are oppressed by degenerate governments. Join our righteous cause and bring the infidels to their knees.* Inspired by having something to live for, along with a clear sense of who the enemy is, idealistic recruits pledge their allegiance to the ideas that spawn terrorism.

What terrorists do on a large scale happens on a small scale every day of our lives. Just as the tiny, harmless-looking Ebola virus can penetrate skin abrasions too small to be seen by the human eye, the virus of conflict seeps in and causes us to feel angry. The president of the National Association of Scholars, Peter Wood, has said the anger epidemic is "more flamboyant, more self-righteous, and more theatrical than anger at other times in our history."[5] We have become, Wood concluded, "a culture that celebrates anger."[6]

Obviously, there's a difference between being angry at others and causing their deaths. Flipping someone the bird in traffic is not the moral equivalent of beheading them. Yet this doesn't get us off the hook. Murder carries a judgment, Jesus said, but "everyone who is angry with his brother will be liable to judgment" as well (Matt. 5:22). In his reply to an early twentieth-century inquiry about what's wrong with the world, English writer and philosopher G. K. Chesterton got straight to the truth: "I am. Yours truly, G. K. Chesterton."[7]

Human conflict runs so deep that some people have given up hope. Physicist Stephen Hawking suggests that our only salvation is to colonize other planets so humanity can't kill itself off all at once. That's an awfully gloomy assessment, but Hawking is not alone in sensing that our survival is at stake. As Ronald Reagan warned, "We'll preserve for our children this, the last best hope of man on Earth, or we'll sentence them to take the last step into a thousand years of darkness." We need answers. Now.

WHERE IS THE ORIGIN OF CONFLICT?

Economists blame scarcity for conflict. We don't have all the time and money we want. We can't get our way. Life is unfair. If we lash out, who can blame us?

A 1997 PBS television special claimed to have identified the culprit: affluenza, defined as a "painful, contagious, socially transmitted condition of overload, debt, anxiety, and waste resulting from the dogged pursuit of more."[8] Bizarrely, some now treat affluenza as an excuse. Attorneys for a Texas teenager claimed that affluenza caused him to drunkenly swerve the car he was driving into a group of people, killing four. He was not guilty of a crime, they argued, because his parents had spoiled him.

Eye-rolling legal arguments aside, philosophers have long sought to understand why we have conflict and how to solve it. In the late 1700s, Jeremy Bentham (1748–1832), founder of the influential philosophy of utilitarianism, said, "Nature has placed mankind under the governance of two sovereign masters, *pain* and *pleasure*."[9] Bentham believed that the best we could do is secure the greatest pleasure and the least amount of pain for the greatest number of people.

What does this look like at a practical level? Bentham proposed a "felicific calculus," an algorithm to measure people's *experience* of happiness. Many political scientists think it is government's job to put this algorithm to good use. Professor Mark Reader wrote, "In the end politics is the place of public happiness."[10] Former Harvard president Derek Bok has said, "In a democracy, you have to be interested in furthering the thing that most people feel is most important to them. And happiness is No. 1, according to the polls."[11] He thinks, for instance, that if government is more aggressive in getting citizens jobs, they will be happier.

If the government (or anyone more powerful than we are) has the power to make us happy but doesn't, then our unhappiness can be blamed on the failure of those more powerful. *The government ought to do something*, people say. But it's a slippery slope. As has been said, a government big enough to give us everything we want is big enough to take everything we have. History's worst mass murderers, such as Stalin, Hitler, and Mao Tse-tung, moved easily from demanding massive restructuring of the government, presumably to benefit people, to killing those who stood in the way.

We want more and we can't obtain it, so someone must be to blame. Who's the culprit? Each of the worldviews we're considering suggests who is at fault and what ought to be done. Here is what they propose.

IDENTIFYING THE LIES COUNTERFEIT WORLDVIEWS TELL ABOUT CONFLICT

We have been examining six worldviews: secularism, Marxism, postmodernism, new spirituality, Islam, and Christianity. We'll look at the first five in this chapter and then explore the Christian worldview in the next chapter.

SECULARISM

Secularism says conflict will cease when we quit worrying about the supernatural and focus on how society disrupts our natural goodness. Novelist Mary Shelley's story about Dr. Victor Frankenstein's creation of a monster provides a starting point for understanding the secular worldview. On an icy mountain slope, Frankenstein comes face to face with the superhuman monster he brought to life—the same monster that has killed those dearest to its creator.

Victor's revulsion is complete: "Abhorred monster," he cries out, "fiend that thou art! The tortures of hell are too mild a vengeance for thy crimes."[12] Frankenstein's monster will have none of it. "I was benevolent and good; misery made me a fiend. Make me happy, and I shall again be virtuous."[13]

Happiness leads to virtue, say secularists, while the absence of happiness transforms benevolent beings into deadly monsters. "Essentially man is internally motivated toward positive personal and social ends," wrote organizational behavior professor Robert Tannenbaum and computer-industry pioneer Sheldon A. Davis in their 1969 article applying secular values to industrial psychology. "The extent to which he is not motivated results from a process of demotivation generated by his relationships and/or environment."[14] In other words, it's society's fault if we're not getting along with one another.

Social psychologist Erich Fromm, in his book *You Shall Be as Gods*, goes so far as to suggest that the concept of sin is itself what keeps us down. When we strip ourselves of outdated notions of

God's will, Fromm argued, we will become positive agents with virtually unlimited potential for good.

Some secularists call for hitting the "reset" button to create a fair society. In a move similar to the Marxist economic plan, which involves taking wealth from the rich and redistributing it to the poor, a popular secular viewpoint insists that *all* of society's goods can be redistributed, including liberty, opportunity, and self-respect. "These principles are the principles of social justice," said the late Harvard professor John Rawls. "They provide a way of assigning rights and duties in the basic institutions of society and they define the appropriate distribution of the benefits and burdens of social cooperation."[15]

POSTMODERNISM

Postmodernism says conflict will cease when we stop pursuing truth. This worldview rejects all metanarratives: the big stories about why things are the way they are. There is no overarching truth that gives meaning to our personal experiences. Conflict is caused by our pretending that *our* metanarrative is the true one.

How far postmodernists will go in blaming metanarratives for causing conflict is revealed in an odd article written in 1991 by French intellectual and postmodern scholar Jean Baudrillard. In "The Gulf War Did Not Take Place," Baudrillard did not deny that bombs were dropped or that people died in the war between Iraq and America and its allies. Rather, he argued that calling the military maneuvers a "war" was a question of how the parties involved defined war, how both Saddam Hussein and the Allied forces used words to get people to see things their way, and how repeatedly played clips of anti-aircraft fire gave the impression that the story the Allied forces were telling was "real." In the end, the intentions of Hussein were not defeated, Baudrillard argued, so the phrase "Gulf War" is not a set of actions that actually took place but a use of rhetoric to describe a particular viewpoint.[16]

Postmodernism says that conflict comes about because in people's pursuit of the truth, they trick others into thinking their position is right. If we all stop pursuing the truth, presumably, conflict will cease.

NEW SPIRITUALITY

New spirituality says conflict will cease when we give up our egos and become one with the universe. Conflict comes from big egos, and big egos come from not understanding our true spiritual power. Spiritual leader Eckhart Tolle has said, "Amazingly but not infrequently, the ego in search of a stronger identity can and does create illnesses in order to strengthen itself through them."[17] When we become aware of our oneness with the universe, all our ego needs—and thus our conflicts—fade away. Indian spiritual teacher Meher Baba declared, "There is only one question. And once you know the answer to that question, there are no more to ask.... Who am I? And to that Question there is only one Answer—I am God!"[18]

We don't need conflict to get what we want, new spirituality says. Popular new age minister Michael Bernard Beckwith has said, "There's more than enough creative ideas. There's more than enough power. There's more than enough love. There's more than enough joy. All of this begins to come through a mind that is aware of its own infinite nature."[19]

So how do you get all these good things? Tolle has put it this way: "You don't have it? Just act as if you had it, and it will come. Then, soon after you start giving, you will start receiving. You cannot receive what you don't give. Outflow determines inflow."[20]

What we're fighting over isn't real, the new spirituality world-view says. When we give up our egos and accept the abundance the universe wants to give us, conflict will go away.

ISLAM

The Quran says conflict will cease when everyone submits to Allah either "willingly or by compulsion."[21] Some believe physical force is a legitimate means to achieve this end. Nabeel Qureshi is a con-vert from Islam to Christianity who upon graduation from medical school became an evangelist rather than a physician. He uses the term *jihadis* to describe those who are committed to using physical violence to achieve the aim of everyone on earth submitting to Allah. By weaponizing their beliefs, jihadis have made themselves into a sort of army that considers legitimate "defense" to include anything that conquers resistance against Islam's becoming a global civilization.[22]

Most Muslims pay little attention to the Quran's warlike com-mands. They might not even know about them. Abdu Murray, a former Muslim, said, "I can't tell you how many Muslims are nominal at best.... If it were a crime to be an orthodox Muslim, they couldn't be convicted of it."[23]

What makes people nervous is that violent jihadis often seem peaceful until just before they attack. Richard Reid seemed like a harmless hippie until he tried to light a bomb in his shoe to bring down a commercial airliner. Germaine Lindsay, the Jamaican convert who blew himself up on a London train and killed twenty-seven people, looked every bit the clean-cut college athlete. Lindsay's wife, Samantha Lewthwaite, smiling like a *Sound of Music* cast member in her INTERPOL photo, is suspected in the deaths of more than four hundred people. This includes the sixty-seven people killed in the Westgate Mall attack in Nairobi.[24] Hasna Aitboulahcen was a cowboy-hat-wearing party girl until she assisted in the 2015 attacks that killed one hundred thirty people in Paris.

Though most Muslims are peace-loving people, the radical beliefs of a tiny yet violent group of jihadis are setting the world on edge. Such religious tension seems like the new normal.

Secularism, postmodernism, new spirituality, and Islam all recognize that something must be done about conflict. The Marxist worldview, though, incorporates conflict into the very way it encourages people to see the world. Look around, the Marxist says. Do you notice how wealth insulates some people from life's troubles, while most people struggle? Why is life so unfair? Marxists say they know precisely what must be done to end the conflict: escalate it.

PEACE ON EARTH, OR ELSE: ISOLATING THE MARXIST WORLDVIEW OF CONFLICT

A recent news item reported that before the opening of a corporate-sponsored Easter egg hunt, a few people slipped through the lines and snagged all the eggs. Because only a certain number of eggs had been hidden, most of those in line were forced to return home empty handed, crying children in tow.

Marxism says society is like that. The wealthy have amassed riches by breaking the rules and taking from the rest of us. Not only that, but they've also managed to get laws enacted that protect their ill-gotten gain. We should take it back, Marxists say, through a democratic vote, if possible, or by force, if necessary. Capitalism must be destroyed, or we will never have peace.

To reduce our pain in the long run, the Marxist says, we must make it worse in the short run. Perhaps you've heard of an idealistic medical student named Ernesto "Che" Guevara, Fidel Castro's right-hand man in his promised democratic socialist government in Cuba. Che's image still adorns T-shirts and posters in places where people feel oppressed. His revolutionary story seems romantic to some, and his death at the hands of the Bolivian army makes him seem saintly. In fact, Che's story became a movie, *The Motorcycle Diaries*, that made him look like a hero who embraced conflict against a few in order to achieve a hopeful future for all.

Do the ends justify the means, as Che believed? Ivan Bahryany, a Ukrainian who estimates that the Soviets killed ten million of his countrymen between 1927 and 1939, stated, "The party clique which follows the slogan expressed by the saying 'the end justifies the means' is actually always ready to use any means."[25] Despite his seemingly good intentions, Che descended from compassion for the poor into outright brutality. With his help, Fidel Castro turned into a dictator who threatened Cuban business owners and confiscated wealth. More than one million people fled the tiny island nation. By the end of his life, Che had founded Cuba's labor camp system and presided over its first firing squads.[26] Thousands were shot—farmers, police officers, business owners, mothers—anyone who was thought to oppose the revolution.

As bad as Cuba was, it was much worse elsewhere. In *The Black Book of Communism*, published by Harvard University Press, Stéphane Courtois wrote that Communist regimes "turned mass crime into a full-blown system of government."[27] In the Soviet Union, this included the execution of tens of thousands of rebellious peasants, man-made famines, and the genocide of uncooperative people groups such as the Cossacks, Ukrainian farmers, the Poles, and the Crimeans.[28] In China, thirty to forty million people died from starvation when military leader Mao Tse-tung seized control of China's farms. A million people were beaten to death by Mao's Red Guards.[29] Twenty million people died in Mao's one thousand labor camps.

The horror spread to other nations too. Two million were systematically killed by the Khmer Rouge regime in Cambodia (at the time called Kampuchea), 1.7 million were worked to death in North Korean labor camps, and 1.1 million were murdered in Yugoslavia, including at least five hundred thousand landlords, business owners, religious leaders, and anti-Communists executed by the Josip Broz Tito regime.[30] The Marxist worldview conquered regions that are home to one-fifth of the world's population, but conflict never ceased.

Marxism promotes a powerful narrative: we suffer because of the selfishness, arrogance, and insensitivity of the rich. Revolution offers long-term gain in exchange for short-term pain, so rather than avoid conflict, we should incite it. The Marxist narrative appeals to those who feel they have little to lose. But history doesn't lie. After a century of Marxist experimentation, we are further than ever from an answer to the question Why can't we get along?

COUNTERFEIT WORLDVIEWS LEAD TO COUNTERFEIT PEACE

Each of the worldviews we've examined outsources the blame for conflict. "It's the fault of the religious." "It's the fault of the rich." "It's the fault of truth seekers." "It's the fault of those who refuse to let go of their individual identities." "It's the fault of those in rebellion against Allah." Conflict won't cease, these worldviews say, until *others* change.

If others must change before conflict ceases, we're stuck with the way things are. Can the Christian worldview offer the breakthrough we seek? This is exactly what a middle-aged World War II military chaplain wondered when he received perhaps the most disturbing assignment ever given to a minister of the gospel: giving spiritual comfort to some of the worst mass murderers in history.

CHAPTER 10

PEACE WINS

How Jesus Offers the Elusive Harmony We All Seek

DECLARATION: I AM MEANT FOR COMMUNITY.
I CAN OVERCOME CONFLICT AND LIVE AT
PEACE WITH THOSE AROUND ME.

Chaplain Henry Gerecke hurried to keep up with a prison guard as the sound of their footsteps echoed off bare walls. Behind the cell doors lining the corridor lived some of the most evil men alive: Nazis who soon would be tried for unspeakable war crimes.

Chaplain Gerecke and his escort arrived at the first cell. Two quick knocks, a key in the lock, then rusty hinges groaned. Suddenly Gerecke stood face to face with Hitler's deputy führer, Rudolf Hess.

He looks like any other man, thought Gerecke as he extended his hand to the prisoner. Hess shook it. Gerecke knew the next day's headline would read, "Army Chaplain Shakes War Criminal's Hand." He didn't care. Hess and the other war criminals needed the gospel. It wasn't Gerecke's job to decide whether the men were guilty before the law. It was his job to pray with them, lead them in services, and counsel them, in the hope that their humanity would be restored and they would be prepared for eternity in light of their likely executions.[1]

In accepting this intimidating assignment, Gerecke committed to carrying out an ancient mission that, in a word, is the secret to restoring what is good when everything has gone bad. This powerful secret proves that we can overcome conflict and live at peace with those around us, even in dire circumstances.

BE INFORMED: "SHALOM" AS THE CHRISTIAN WORLDVIEW RESPONSE TO CONFLICT

A secret battle of ideas rages over the origin of conflict and what to do about it. The Christian worldview's approach may be summarized in one word: *shalom*. This simple Hebrew term unfolds into a world of meanings: peace, wellness, soundness, welfare, prosperity, tranquility, and contentment. Shalom describes what life together looks like in a world God has redeemed. *Shalom* is a word that captures broken community becoming unbroken.

This stands apart from the way other worldviews consider conflict, which is that conflict is the fault of "those people": the religious, the rich, truth seekers, those who insist on maintaining an individual identity, or those who resist Allah's laws. Shalom replaces this approach. Here are three insights about how.

INSIGHT #1: SHALOM ACKNOWLEDGES THE CONFLICT *INSIDE* US AS WELL AS *AMONG* US

Although there are people who stand for evil and must be opposed, there is no "us" versus "them." Every person bears God's image and possesses a soul that will live for eternity. We're all here for a reason. As has been said, there are no passengers on the ship of life, only crew. Shalom is a whole way of life focused on unity rather than division.

INSIGHT #2: SHALOM FOCUSES ON *GIVING* RATHER THAN *TAKING*

A "me first," Darwinian mind-set will never arrive at shalom. You can receive it only as you give it to others. In ancient times, the prophet Jeremiah told the captive Jews living in Babylon that their shalom would be secured as they worked to secure it for those around them (see Jer. 29:7). Instructing God's people to heal their communities rather than separate from them is an extraordinary thing to tell war captives, and it is echoed in Paul's admonition to "bless and … not curse" (Rom. 12:14).

INSIGHT #3: SHALOM FOCUSES ON *LOVE*, NOT *HATE*

Jesus declared, "You have heard that it was said, 'You shall love your neighbor and hate your enemy.' But I say to you, Love your enemies and pray for those who persecute you" (Matt. 5:43–44).

This is shalom in action: responding gracefully without compromise. If you've been to Israel, you may have received a *shalom aleichem* greeting from a Jewish person. It's a simple yet powerful greeting, wishing you to experience God's richest blessings in life's everyday moments. This is the kind of love that comes from God. It's what children's author Sally Lloyd-Jones has described as a "Never Stopping, Never Giving Up, Unbreaking, Always and Forever Love."

Shalom acknowledges the conflicts that rage inside us as well as among us. It focuses on giving rather than taking and calls for love rather than hate. The nature of shalom, as well as the approach it takes, makes its vision of conflict unique. So why don't we all live in peace? In the secret battle we face, idea viruses threaten shalom, a lesson I learned as I grew up in one of America's most troubled cities.

HOW JESUS'S PEACE DEFEATS THE IDEA VIRUS OF CONFLICT

I watched from the living room window. Two attendants wheeled a stretcher out the front door of a house across the street. A white sheet covered what was unmistakably a human form. Something was very wrong.

"What are they doing, Mom?" I asked.

"They're taking the person into the ambulance," she explained, not sure how to tell a seven-year-old what really was happening.

"But why is the person covered up?"

"Honey, the person did not live."

"Why not?"

"Well," she replied, fumbling for words, "I think the person took some drugs."

This terrified me. Just a few days before, an older kid on a street corner had offered my friend and me some pills. We refused. I knew drugs were bad, but I had no idea they could kill you.

Drugs had become a way of life in 1970s Detroit. So had muggings and shootings. It was a city fallen from grace. During its heyday in the 1950s, Detroit was one of the most prosperous cities in the world, with a population of 1.8 million people, art deco architecture, and neatly kept neighborhoods.

In 1967, though, racial tensions boiled over into riots. Forty-three people died in the violence that year, more than one thousand were injured, and nearly fourteen hundred buildings were burned. As I grew older, I sensed the fear. One evening outside our house, police shot at an escaping thief who had crashed a stolen car into my dad's vanilla-white Volkswagen Beetle, which was parked along the curb. I hid under my bed and prayed that I would never have to come out.

Today, even after many restarts, Detroit is a shell of its former self. More than half the property owners failed to pay property taxes in 2011.[2] *Forbes* magazine lists Detroit as the most dangerous city in America.[3] The artery of trust has hemorrhaged. To this, shalom offers both good news and bad news. The bad news is that shalom has been violated. The good news is that it can be restored.

SHALOM HAS BEEN VIOLATED

The secret battle of ideas attacks community. Residents of American cities routinely face crime, congestion, ineffective schools, dilapidated housing, lack of adequate services, homelessness, and corruption. Abortion on demand, dignity-stripping overdependence on welfare, and fatherlessness plague the urban poor. One in four American youths is at serious risk of not achieving productive adulthood.[4] No one can predict accurately whether at-risk youth will go to college or jail.

Shalom has been violated. But this is not the end of the story.

SHALOM CAN BE RESTORED

The Christian worldview says Christ's sacrifice doesn't just bandage things up so we can limp through life; it restores fullness and wholeness to life, both now and forever.[5] But the idea viruses of conflict say shalom is a faded vision, a remnant of a world that no longer exists. Until others get their act together, peace is impossible. Shalom disagrees. It says that change starts with me. It's a lesson I learned in a difficult conversation with my father.

"Dad, can we talk?"

"Sure," my father said, looking over from the steering wheel, confused. We had been talking for hours as we passed through Oklahoma on the way to Texas, where I would be going to school.

I quickly clarified, "I mean about some hard things I think we need to talk about."

He nodded.

My hands shook as I looked down at the piece of paper on which I had scratched some notes. I was barely in my twenties at the time. Four years earlier, when I had left for college, my relationship with my dad had been awful. Once, I called home to tell him I planned to join a fraternity. "Well, I'm just going to give you over to your own lusts," he said. What? It sounded to me like bizarre-Christian-workshop talk. But I had stopped caring. I was tired of feeling that I couldn't do anything right.

All that changed in an instant in a car crash. My little Volkswagen Beetle was struck broadside and thrown into a tree, the impact fracturing bones in my neck. During the required surgery and extensive recuperation, my dad helped nurse me back to health. When I could work again, he gave me a job. The chill between us began to melt.

For some reason, I had decided that the drive to Texas would be the right time to try to reach closure. "Dad, I want to confess to you the things I have done that I know disappointed you, and I want to share the things you've done that hurt me."

Another nod.

I read through my list. My dad didn't say anything. Then, without warning, he steered our big Buick station wagon onto the shoulder and got out, hands on his hips, staring into the distance.

I got out and stood beside him. Turning his tearstained face toward me, he said simply, "Son, I am so sorry."

"I am too, Dad."

We hugged. By this point, my mother had gotten out of the back seat and put her arms around both of us. Years of tension dissolved.

As we embraced, an Oklahoma Department of Transportation truck slowed, then cautiously pulled in front of us. A head poked out of a side window. "Y'all okay? We can get help. No need to worry or nothin'." We assured him we were fine, and a few minutes later we resumed our journey. But there, on the side of a highway in the hot Oklahoma sun, shalom had been restored. What might that kind of shalom look like for our distraught culture?

SHALOM RESTORES WHAT WAS LOST IN THE FALL

Shalom doesn't just deal with conflict. It transcends it with a clear, positive picture of what peace looks like and how to achieve it, painted with three bold colors.

SHALOM RESTORES COMMUNITY

At the heart of shalom is what journalist Andy Crouch called the "flourishing of exquisitely relational creatures" who "bear the image of a relational God."[6] Genesis 1:27 says that God made human beings in his image and likeness. God relates to us personally. He's not just a force to energize us through some superspecial electrical current, nor is he a distant deity who broadcasts a list of laws we must obey. His life reaches to our lives.

By its very nature, shalom flowers through personal presence. It can't be dictated by people in a far-off capital, no matter how well-meaning those people are. It can't be waved into existence by positive thoughts, nor is it well served by lists of religious rules.

No, shalom comes to us as we live in community with one another. This is what church is for. The state ought to secure justice, but it is the church that knows why justice exists in the first place. The government can and ought to enforce laws against stealing, but it is the church that explains that stealing violates shalom, upsetting the trust people feel when they're safe and secure.

SHALOM RESTORES THE NEWNESS WE HAD IN CREATION

Shalom says that things being *made new* is better than their being new in the first place. Earlier today, before I began writing, I saw a beautifully restored vanilla-white Volkswagen Beetle, just like the one my father drove before it was destroyed by a car thief. It was old, but it looked brand new. Its value was probably far more than its original price because of its rarity and the immense labor of love that had restored it to its original condition.

Shalom is a vision for making things better than new. I once saw a gracious leader handle a personal attack by saying, "I'm afraid I'm really much worse than you think. I'm a flawed person God has chosen to advance this vision. I accept your criticism and commit to learning from it and doing better next time." My respect for him grew; here was a leader restored to his original condition, but better.

Shalom affects everything, even our personal health. In 1948, alarmed that cardiovascular disease was the leading cause of death in America, researchers recruited 5,209 men and women in Framingham, Massachusetts, to undergo physical testing and to complete lifestyle questionnaires. Using data from this ongoing study, researchers at Harvard University found that, on average, for every contented person each of the people in the study knew, their own likelihood of being content increased by 2 percent. For every discontented person they knew, their likelihood of being discontent rose by 4 percent. In other words, unhappy people are twice as damaging to one's state of mind as happy people are good for it.[7] And happier people are healthier people! Our very bodies were created for shalom.

SHALOM RESTORES COMMUNICATION

Shalom says a good talk is one of the best things that can happen. There's a powerful word in English to describe a good talk: *dialogue*. The word *dialogue* comes from two Greek words, *dia* (through) and *logos* (word/thought). To dialogue is to talk through thoughts. The apostle John begins his gospel account by saying that Jesus is the Word: the *logos* of God. When we dialogue, we communicate the way God communicates.

Idea viruses often compel us to use talk to build ourselves up. MIT professor William Isaacs admitted, "Often I lie in wait in meetings, like a hunter looking for his prey, ready to spring out at the first moment of silence. My gun is loaded with preestablished thoughts. I take aim and fire, the context irrelevant, my bullet and its release all that matter to me."[8]

Dialogue helps immunize us to this kind of talk. Isaacs defined dialogue as "a *conversation with a center, not sides*."[9] Dialogue helps people understand one another in a way that helps them act in an entirely new fashion.[10] This is shalom in action. It thinks first. It describes rather than accuses. It focuses on getting a good outcome, not "going off." It avoids words and topics that trigger unhelpful responses. Asking "Is this conversation building shalom?" brings clarity and focus to our talk.

Shalom changes the way we communicate, helping us look out for one another, seek one another's best interests, and become friends. We need this, especially in a time when deep friendships are becoming rarer[11] and texting and social media connect us but leave us even lonelier and more anxious.[12]

INVEST IN YOURSELF AND OTHERS: FOUR THINGS TO DO RIGHT NOW TO EXPERIENCE JESUS'S PEACE

Why can't we all get along? Shalom is the Christian worldview's answer. We are to "live peaceably with all" (Rom. 12:18) and "not become conceited, provoking one another, envying one another" (Gal. 5:26). But what should we do differently?

1. Replace anger with patience. Shalom is most needed where there is anger, whether it is a community-wide problem, such as racial tension, or a personal problem, such as coworkers who can't stand one another. Personally, I find that my impatience, combined with my hatred of conflict, makes me want to get conflict over with quickly, even if rushing through it leads to a bad outcome. As I learn about shalom, however, I'm learning to wait, whether it is a few hours or a few days, until the Holy Spirit adjusts my attitude. I'm discovering the meaning of James 1:19, which says, "Let every person be quick to hear, slow to speak, slow to anger."

2. See God's image in others. In the midst of conflict, it's easy to diminish others. First Corinthians 13:4, though, says that "love is patient and kind." Those I might find myself in conflict with are made in God's image. God thought them through. He loves them very much. Imagine that someone walks up to your child and launches into a harshly worded lecture. You'd be offended, even if the person's criticism is technically accurate, because your child is of your very nature and in your image. We can imagine that God sees his children in a similar way.

3. Be a peacemaker, not just a peacekeeper. Shalom isn't just about avoiding conflict; it's also about actively seeking to bring peace between people. A college student told me that she dreaded going to class because her professor seemed cranky and easily angered. When she tried to show him respect, it just seemed to make him angrier. Yet she knew that God had placed her there to restore shalom. I suggested she say something such as "Professor, I sense that sometimes I rub you the wrong way. I want you to know that I appreciate your leadership. I want to learn and grow in your class. It means a lot to me that you take pains to involve us. And even when we're not thoughtful, you are patient in helping us learn."

4. Never lose hope. Before suffering on the cross, Jesus prayed for his disciples to experience oneness so everyone could know that God the Father sent Jesus and loved them even as he loved his Son (see John 17:23). The way of Jesus comes to the fore in our ability to find common ground. Through God's mercy, we are rescued from self-destruction and enabled to love. Others might never change, but the way we approach others absolutely changes us.

Shalom is quick to listen and slow to become angry because anger doesn't bring what God wants. Shalom humbly recognizes that as fellow image bearers of God, our well-being is tied to the well-being of others. This is why shalom pursues peace rather than just avoiding conflict. Shalom portrays conflict as two people standing side by side, facing a common enemy, rather than head to head, making enemies out of each other. As we understand shalom, we can grasp how Chaplain Henry Gerecke managed to minister to some of the most violent, hate-filled, evil men in history.

ONE MORE THING

Henry Gerecke's congregants were thugs, no doubt about it. But Gerecke knew that restoring shalom involved inviting these men to rejoin humanity before they faced their eternal destiny. At last, after months of ministry, the verdicts were announced. Eleven of

Gerecke's congregants at the Nuremberg prison had received the death sentence. Ten were hanged, and one, Hermann Göring, committed suicide.

What I found shocking in Gerecke's account was this: before their deaths, many had repented of their sins and trusted Jesus Christ as their savior. If this is true, there will be Nazi war criminals in heaven. I find that hard to imagine, but from God's perspective it's not hard at all. Truth isn't just a concept; it's a person sent to rescue us. Love isn't just an idea; it's a life given in our place. Shalom isn't just a word; it is *the* Word. And in this, there is hope that our deepest imperfections can become our greatest strengths and that the things that divide us can, through a power greater than our own, create a unity more profound than we could ever manufacture. This is how we each can declare freedom from idea viruses that keep us miserably trapped in conflict: *I am meant for community. I can overcome conflict and live at peace with those around me.*

Yet, unfortunately, hopelessness still grows. Despair descends on us like a plague. Is there any hope for us personally and for civilization itself? One entrepreneur thinks he knows how hope might be restored: by blasting people off into space.

CHAPTER 11

IS THERE ANY HOPE FOR THE WORLD?

How Idea Viruses Drive Us to Despair

If you've ever wanted to travel into space, entrepreneur Sir Richard Branson thinks in a few years he'll be able to get you there. It will cost you, though. With tickets at $250,000 each, Branson's space-travel program promises a six-minute view of planet earth from sixty-eight miles above its surface.[1] It's clearly a bucket-list item for the very wealthy, but Branson thinks it's a joyride that will change your life. Lots of people agree. Already, seven hundred paying passengers have made reservations, including Justin Bieber, Ashton Kutcher, and Paris Hilton. If the hundreds of potential passengers were to make the trip, they would more than double the number of people who have been in space.

Imagine being given a seat on the Virgin Galactic spaceship. The company's website asks readers to envision "a wave of unimaginable but controlled power" as the rocket accelerates out of the earth's atmosphere at three times the speed of sound. When the craft reaches its arc, the engine shuts down and those aboard unbuckle and float around the cabin, free from gravity. They gaze out windows at the earth without marked boundaries, ribboned by a fragile atmosphere. "What you are looking at is the source of everything it means to be human," says the website, "and it is home."[2]

In some ways, seeing the planet from space must be a relief. For a brief time, you wouldn't encounter starvation or crime or violence. You wouldn't feel the pain of those undergoing chemotherapy or the fear of those cowering underneath a table as mortar shells scream overhead. Cruelty and neglect and egomania are so distant that they seem insignificant. For six minutes you'd have hope. But then your craft would return to earth, right back to all the troubles humans face.

Is there any hope for the world—hope that lasts longer than a few minutes of an exhilarating experience? We humans have been asking the question for a long time, and we're still waiting for an answer. Proverbs 13:12 says, "Hope deferred makes the heart sick." We're afflicted by the virus of despair, and it is spreading fast. A review of eighty-nine studies that administered the Beck Hopelessness Scale, a psychological scale that measures people's hope for the future, motivations, and expectations, found that hopefulness has declined in the last three decades. The study also found that American students are significantly less hopeful than students around the world.[3]

At some point, people will give up completely, and we seem to be approaching that point very quickly. Do any of the worldviews we're considering offer hope for us personally and for civilization as a whole?

IS THERE ANY HOPE?

Before the modern age, human life was "nasty, brutish, and short," as English philosopher Thomas Hobbes famously described it.[4] Yet by the end of the 1800s, according to author Sylvia Nasar in *Grand Pursuit*, the Western world had undergone an extraordinary change of worldview. People discovered that their "circumstances were not predetermined, immutable, or utterly impervious to human intervention."[5]

Discovering that civilization was not bound by fate, humans achieved greater advances in a century than in the previous five thousand years. Observing the seeming march to utopia, historian J. B. Bury enthused that the idea of progress "belongs to the same order of ideas as Providence or personal immortality."[6] Who needs God? Progress is inevitable. Heaven on earth is almost here.

Within fourteen years of the dawn of the twentieth century, however, humanity began receiving a shocking and prolonged wake-up call. World War I claimed thirty-eight million lives. The Bolshevik revolution in Russia capitalized on the chaos, unleashing the idea virus of communism, which ultimately claimed more than a hundred million lives and inflicted unimaginable suffering around the globe.[7] To make matters worse, in 1918 and 1919, the Spanish flu pandemic caused fifty million deaths.

Just three decades into what people thought would be the dawning of a hopeful new era, the twentieth century was already the bloodiest century in human history. And that was twenty years before the advent of World War II, in which another sixty million people lost their lives. It's hard to conceive of death on such a scale. Imagine everyone in the United States east of the Mississippi River being killed, plus all of Canada.

Looking back at the early decades of the twentieth century, psychologist Erich Fromm wrote, "In the nineteenth century the problem was that *God is dead*; in the twentieth century the problem is that *man is dead*."[8] In the midst of the heartache, Fromm questioned what it even meant to be human.

The opposite of hope is despair, which famed mystery author Dorothy L. Sayers described as the deadly sin that punishes us for all the other sins. It is, she wrote memorably, "the sin that believes in nothing, cares for nothing, seeks to know nothing, interferes with nothing, enjoys nothing, loves nothing, hates nothing, finds purpose in nothing, lives for nothing, and remains alive only because there is nothing it would die for."[9]

Humanity had sown the wind and reaped the whirlwind. As the band Green Day sang, we're lost on the boulevard of broken dreams:

> My shadow's the only one that walks beside me;
> My shallow heart's the only thing that's beating.
> Sometimes I wish someone out there will find me;
> 'Til then I walk alone.[10]

Sometimes the world seems like a giant crime scene. We're tempted to wrap it in yellow tape and walk away, hoping that some cosmic detective can gather all the clues and prosecute those responsible. But there's no place to walk away to. This side of eternity, the world is our home, though it might not last much longer, according to the Center for Ecoliteracy: "Fossil fuels, groundwater, forests, minerals, cropland soils, marine fisheries, and other natural resources are being depleted much more quickly than they can be replenished."[11] If any of us is to survive, we need drastic action, the thinking goes. Paul Watson, founder of the Sea Shepherd Conservation Society, called for the human population to be reduced to fewer than one billion (from more than seven billion), saying, "Curing a body of cancer requires radical and invasive therapy, and therefore, curing the biosphere of the human virus will also require a radical and invasive approach."[12]

This is crazy. Can it be true that our only hope is to extinguish ourselves? Let's look at what each worldview says, leaving the Islamic worldview's hard-hitting solution for last.

IDENTIFYING THE LIES COUNTERFEIT WORLDVIEWS TELL ABOUT HOPE

Counterfeit worldviews don't just give up in the face of despair. They can't. Otherwise, people would never embrace them. Each worldview must give us a reason to keep going. Here's what the advocates of each worldview say.

SECULARISM

To the worldview of secularism, the Christian view that people are the most beautiful thing on earth because we are image bearers of God is foolish talk, even dangerous. Our existence is nothing special. E. A. Burtt, a philosopher who was the son of missionaries to China and later rejected his faith, said gloomily, "The ultimate accommodation necessary in a wise plan of life is acceptance of a world not made for man, owing him nothing, and in its major processes quite beyond his control."[13]

Secularism, as you remember, says that the material world is all there is. Our brains are, as artificial-intelligence pioneer Marvin Minsky bluntly phrased it, computers made out of meat.[14] Life is what we make it, and when it's over, it's over. Georgetown professor Jacques Berlinerblau said, "The secularish are here-and-now people. They live for this world, not for the next."[15]

So where is the hope? It's in the possibility that humans are smart enough to scrape together our own plan of salvation. British evolutionary biologist Julian Huxley wrote, "Man's destiny is to be the sole agent for the future evolution of this planet."[16] Secularists talk about this kind of thing a lot. Many are hoping technology will save us. Oxford philosopher Nick Bostrom suggested that technology will ultimately become so advanced that we will become "posthuman," essentially ensuring that all our human limitations can be overcome.[17]

Where is God in this? Nowhere, the secularist says. In the "Humanist Manifesto II," philosopher Paul Kurtz put it this way: "No deity will save us; we must save ourselves."[18] Kurtz's publishing company even offers a children's book to strip the young of the illusion that hope may be found in God. It reads in part, "A god is a mythical character. Mythical characters are imaginary, they're not real. People make them up. Dragons and fairies are two of many mythical characters people have made up. They're not real."[19]

Good-bye, dragons. Good-bye, fairies. Good-bye, Jesus.

MARXISM

Marxism holds that, at root, it is the rich who have destroyed our hope through what Karl Marx referred to as their "naked, shameless, direct, brutal exploitation."[20] There is no salvation aside from their overthrow.[21] "The philosophers have only *interpreted* the world in various ways," Marx stated. "The point, however, is to *change* it."[22]

According to Marx, we can restore hope by raising taxes and confiscating property until wealth is redistributed and economic classes no longer exist. It must be done now. Anyone who calls for patience is one of the oppressors. Author and social activist bell hooks (intentionally not capitalized), whom *Essence* magazine called a "visionary feminist,"[23] wove impatience into virtually every line of her jarring prose. Forget the future, hooks said in a college commencement speech; we need change now. Anything else is "a form of psychic violence" that benefits "every imperialist, white supremacist, capitalist, patriarchal nation on the planet."[24]

Redemption isn't what we need, according to Marxism. It's too ambiguous and frustratingly slow. Revolution is laser sharp and thrillingly fast. It's our only hope.

POSTMODERNISM

Postmodernism asserts that universal truth cannot be known; we can know only whether our individual experiences are true for us.[25] So forget the idea of taking control or sparking revolution, postmodernism says. The world is too fragmented and complex for such solutions. Those who disagree are just trying to rig the rules of the game to benefit themselves.

People aren't the problem, postmodernism says, but nor are they the solution. In fact, there really isn't such a thing as a person. We might be subjects or bodies or units, but to say that humans have a personal nature is to proclaim something we can't possibly know to be true.[26]

Perhaps it goes without saying, but a world devoid of ultimate meaning and purpose doesn't inspire hope. It can't even make a coherent worldview. Even if it could, there would be no point, as there would be no way to know whether it were true.

NEW SPIRITUALITY

Unlike secularism, Marxism, and postmodernism, new spirituality says our problems are spiritual, not physical. Spiritual teacher Deepak Chopra said, "All around us people ache with emptiness and yearning; there's a vacuum to be filled, and it's a spiritual vacuum. What other word really fits? Only when people are given hope that this ache can be healed will we truly know what the future holds."[27]

For a growing number of spiritual teachers, business consultants, bestselling authors, and television hosts, hope comes from rejecting traditional religion and embracing our divinity, power, and godlikeness. We are one with the universe. When we begin acting as though we are one with everything, the world will change.

Advocates of new spirituality think embracing our divinity is the solution for the world because of what they think the world is actually like. Only the spiritual world is real; everything else is an illusion. We humans are conscious of this, which makes us special. The way forward, new spirituality says, is through searching for *higher* consciousness, which is sort of like "The Force" that Obi-Wan Kenobi described to Luke Skywalker in *Star Wars*: "It's an energy field created by all living things. It surrounds us and penetrates us; it binds the galaxy together."[28]

The new-spirituality worldview says everything is one. If we call this oneness "God," then everything is God, including you and me. Proclaiming ourselves to be gods seems like an awfully pompous thing to do, though. Some new-spirituality teachers recognize this as a problem. According to Eckhart Tolle, enlightenment comes when we rid ourselves of ego rather than inflate it. The world, he says, is "preparing the ground for a more profound shift in planetary consciousness that is destined to take place in the human species."[29] Losing our sense of self and melting into the oneness of all life is what will give us hope.

To recap, each worldview offers a different take on what brings hope. The secular worldview says hope comes when humans learn to direct the course of evolution to make the world a better place for all its inhabitants. Marxism says hope arises as we muster our courage and overthrow the structures of society that keep us down. Postmodernism, while accepting the idea that only the material world exists, disagrees with secularism and Marxism because no "big story" of the world—no metanarrative—can bring us the hope we need. In fact, it's not even clear who "we" are. New spirituality takes a very different tack than secularism, Marxism, and postmodernism. It says the material world is an illusion. Everything is spiritual. The universe wants what is good for us. Becoming one with it will bring us hope.

Although very different from one another, each of these views proposes something we must do, some action we must take, to restore hope. Islam, on the other hand, insists that hope will arise when we stop doing something: rebelling against Allah.

SQUELCHING THE REBELLION: ISOLATING THE ISLAMIC WORLDVIEW'S IDEA OF HOPE

Most Westerners misunderstand radical Islam's hope for the world. That is the conclusion drawn by two respected scholars of Islam in an article published in *Foreign Policy* magazine. Radical Muslims are not terrorizing the world because they are poor and uneducated, the scholars wrote. Quite the opposite. Radicals earn more money and stay in school longer than moderates, and they express more satisfaction with their financial situation.[30]

So why are radical Muslims lashing out? It's because they believe that the Western world is a threat to the only thing they think will bring hope: unquestioning obedience to Allah.

Islam is a totalistic worldview. You can't pick and choose the parts you like and still be a faithful Muslim. Urbain Vermeulen, former president of the European Union of Arabists and Islamicists, stated simply, "In Islam you can't eat *à la carte*, you have to take the whole menu."[31]

The Islamic worldview begins with Muhammad's teaching that every human is born a Muslim in a state of submission to Allah. From very young ages, though, we are led astray to worship false gods or to deny God altogether. Mercifully, the Islamic worldview says, Allah sent prophets to speak to the nations and correct these errors of belief and practice (see Quran 16:36; 35:24). Moses and Jesus—as well as Ishmael, Isaac, and Jacob—are considered prophets of Islam (see Quran 61:6; 2:136). Of all the prophets, though, Muhammad is seen as the best (see Quran 33:40).

Islam often is compared with Judaism and Christianity, but its basic teachings are quite different. Muhammad taught that we are not God's image bearers; we are not his sons and daughters. Rather, the Quran says, we are his slaves. We have only one responsibility, and that is to follow God's law. Feeling close to God is irrelevant. We can know him only through obedience.[32]

Hope arises in an Islamic worldview when people cease their rebellion against Allah. This happens through jihad, which, as we saw in earlier chapters, is the battle for self-discipline and resisting anything that hinders the advance of Islam.[33] Fighting against non-Muslims is viewed not as an act of aggression but as a way of offering Allah's mercy to those who are willing to end their rebellious ways.

Many Islamic regimes interpret jihad aggressively, pressuring nonbelievers, especially Christians, to convert to Islam or undergo tremendous hardship, even death. They envision a global Islamic state—a theocracy—ruled by religious leaders according to the principles of Sharia law.[34] This leads to widespread persecution that is intensifying, according to a comprehensive study of global persecution.[35] Radical Muslims don't see it that way, however. They feel that if nonbelievers would just quit being stubborn and submit to Allah, their faithfulness would be welcomed with open arms. Hope would be restored for all.

COUNTERFEIT WORLDVIEWS LEAD TO COUNTERFEIT HOPE

We started out with the question "Is there any hope for the world?" Secularism, Marxism, postmodernism, new spirituality, and Islam each provide different answers regarding what we need to do or stop doing. According to each, we can discipline ourselves to act differently and solve our own problems. In our strength we place our hope.

But in a world of idea viruses, just being strong is sometimes a weakness. In chapter 2, I mentioned the Spanish flu, which killed tens of millions of people in the early twentieth century. Unlike other forms of the flu, the Spanish flu didn't just pick on the physically infirm. Like the Ebola virus, it killed its victims by tricking the immune system into overreacting. The stronger the immune system, the more devastating the response to the virus. In some ways, the strength of the healthy made them more frail.

Often, in society, the appearance of strength covers a fault line deep within the culture. When things shift, destruction occurs quickly and without warning. As historian Will Durant wrote in his analysis of the peasant wars in England, "From barbarism to civilization requires a century; from civilization to barbarism needs but a day."[36]

Is it possible that our own strength is not enough to restore hope? Might the true path to strength be through weakness? To answer those questions, let's join a courageous journalist as she rides into the heart of terrorist country—gun-waving driver at the wheel—to figure out how people who have nothing left to live for still have hope in the midst of their dire circumstances.

CHAPTER 12

HOPE ENDURES

How Jesus Restores Hope in the Midst of Despair

DECLARATION: THERE IS HOPE FOR THE WORLD. I AM NOT DOOMED. WHAT IS RIGHT AND JUST AND TRUE WILL WIN.

Nearing the Iraqi city of Mosul, with its checkpoints and soldiers armed with machine guns, Mindy Belz pulled out her scarf and formed it into a hijab, twisting its ends around her neck. Seated in the back seat of a car, she smoothed her skirt down over her knees, avoiding the gaze of the men who walked along the dust-choked road.

Her traveling companion passed a gun to the driver, who clenched it in his left hand while driving with his right, accelerating toward the heart of the city. A journalist, Mindy scribbled observations in her notebook. "Go together. Go fast," she wrote.

Gazing out the window, Mindy was horrified at how much Mosul had deteriorated since her last visit five years earlier. There was litter everywhere. Gravel berms topped with razor wire lined the roads. Once-bustling parks were closed. Restaurants were boarded up. A Ferris wheel sat in a weed-choked lot, unmoving, abandoned.

What on earth am I doing here? Mindy wondered. She was a mom and a wife. But she also was a journalist. There was a war on, and people needed to know what was happening.

Mindy sensed that a bigger story was forming, a story of despair and hope, and she would be the one to tell it. Mindy learned that in war-devastated Iraq, the withdrawal of US troops had left a power vacuum that was filled by a ruthless warlord named Abu Bakr al-Baghdadi. Al-Baghdadi believed that it pleased Allah to enslave, kill, and rape Christians. His band of thugs, called ISIS by Westerners, had swelled to an army of thirty thousand men.

With her firsthand perspective and personal contacts, Mindy was no longer just a war correspondent; she was the world's link to a humanitarian crisis of enormous proportions. It was her job— no, her *mission*—to unflinchingly tell the big stories of cities being destroyed and millions of Christians and other minorities being kidnapped, driven out, and killed.[1] But there were little stories to tell as well: believers cheerfully sharing their meager provisions, a priest with multiple sclerosis shuffling around refugee camps to minister to the afflicted, and people caring for the disabled and wounded when they could barely care for themselves.

As I listened to Mindy's stories and read them in her book *They Say We Are Infidels*, I couldn't help but ask, *Where is hope in a world that seems so dark?* Our conversation, which I'll share in this chapter, started me on a surprising journey to grasp how hope secures victory in the secret battle of ideas, freeing me from idea viruses that reinforced my sense of impending doom and offering hope that what is right and just and true will win.

BE INFORMED: "ELPIS" AS THE CHRISTIAN WORLDVIEW RESPONSE TO DESPAIR

It's easy to lose hope. In J. R. R. Tolkien's *The Fellowship of the Ring*, Haldir the Elf said, "The world is indeed full of peril, and in it there are many dark places."[2] Evil marches on, and it often seems the good will never win. If you're discouraged, here are two insights that could restore your hope.

INSIGHT #1: WITHOUT GOD IN THE EQUATION, HOPE SEEMS LIKE A PARADOX

Every worldview has a story about what evil is, where it came from, and what hope we have of vanquishing it. According to Greek mythology, evil was released into the world through a vengeful trick. Angered by the Titan Prometheus's having stolen fire from heaven, Zeus, the ruler of the gods, fashioned a lovely, charming woman endowed with the habits of a thief—deceit and flattery—and gave her to Prometheus's brother Epimetheus. The woman's name was Pandora.

Pandora arrived on Epimetheus's doorstep with a jar. Against his better judgment, Epimetheus took her in. When he did so,

Pandora opened the jar, releasing all manner of evil, toil, and disease. The Greek poet Hesiod wrote,

> Among the people wander countless miseries;
> the earth is full of evils, and the sea is full;
> diseases come by day to people,
> and by night, spontaneous, rushing,
> bringing mortals evil things.[3]

But not everything was released from Pandora's jar. One thing alone remained trapped inside: *elpis*. It's the Greek word for hope. Hope is trapped by a paradox: it exists only as long as it never appears, yet its absence drives us to despair.

INSIGHT #2: WITH GOD IN THE EQUATION, HOPE IS REAL AND WE CAN HAVE IT

The same word used for hope in the myth of Pandora, *elpis*, also is used in places such as Ephesians 1:18, where Paul wishes for his hearers to have the eyes of their hearts enlightened so they may know the hope to which they were called.

From God's perspective, hope is the expectation that something good will happen, that a better day will arrive. Hope runs on a parallel track with faith: "Faith is the confidence that what we hope for will actually happen," said the author of Hebrews (11:1 NLT).

But for many worldviews, hope is far off. The counterfeit worldviews we've looked at teach that nothing will change unless everything changes: *only* the abolition of religion will bring enlightenment; *only* a worldwide revolution will solve the poverty problem; *only* when the globe's population learns to meditate on higher consciousness will utopia arrive.

To these worldviews, there is only the thinnest of possibilities that hope will be realized. Not so with the Christian worldview, and for three surprising reasons.

HOW JESUS'S HOPE DEFEATS THE IDEA VIRUS OF DESPAIR

I stood there at the top of what seemed like an icy cliff. It shouldn't have been that scary. Lots of people, including small children, were zooming past me. But I was terrified.

Just two years prior to this, I had narrowly escaped paralysis after suffering a broken neck in a car accident. My doctor had instructed me not to go water-skiing, horseback riding, or downhill skiing. "Everyone else gets second chances," he said. "But with the fused bones in your neck, you won't." Yet here I was, having accepted free ski lessons at one of Colorado's famous resorts. *This is a very, very bad idea*, I thought. But it was too late. There was only one way down.

Tearing my attention away from the slope, I heard my instructor say, "You're going to feel like the slope is your enemy. You'll feel like leaning back and shying away from it. But leaning back makes your skis harder to control. The only way to do this is to lean into the thing you're afraid of."

So down I went. Leaning in. It was glorious. Don't tell my doctor, but I've come to enjoy downhill skiing. Yet each time I go, I remind myself, *Lean in—it's the only way.*

Hope is like that. We are going down the slope of life. Our choice is either to shy away in fear or to lean in to hope. The Christian worldview is one of hope. We are not doomed. What is right and just and true will win. That's why we're not like those who grieve because they have no hope (see 1 Thess. 4:13). Instead, we can live fearlessly, resiliently, and confidently.

HOPE HELPS US LIVE FEARLESSLY

I recently journeyed through a season of depression. In the midst of it, I felt locked in fear and indecision. I lost hope in the future. Each morning as I awoke to face another day, my conversations with Jesus seemed to go like this:

> "Jesus, I can't imagine living this way for months and years."
> "Jeff, let's not live months and years. Let's live today."
> "But, Jesus, I don't think I can even do today."
> "That's okay. Can you make it to lunchtime?"
> "Yes, I think I can."
> "Okay, let's go. I'm right here beside you."

Fear is not overcome by "no fear." Fear is overcome by the close presence of the One whose strength created the world and everything in it. Fear is strong, but God is stronger (see Isa. 41:10). Fear is overcome by love (see 1 John 4:18). We do not have a spirit of fear but one of power and love and self-control (see 2 Tim. 1:7). We are overcomers as Jesus takes command of what makes us afraid. As we have seen in previous chapters, Jesus overcomes hate and turns it into love. He overcomes suffering and turns it into victory. He overcomes meaninglessness and turns it into calling. He overcomes conflict and turns it into peace.

HOPE HELPS US LIVE RESILIENTLY

To bestselling author and risk analyst Nassim Nicholas Taleb, there's bad news and there's worse news. The bad news is that shocking, terrible things are going to happen in the world. It's a statistical inevitability. The worse news is that most people are completely unprepared. They're fragile. They're just a few mistakes away from losing it all.

So how should you respond? Taleb said the worst thing you can do is try to protect yourself by armoring up, like turtles whose hard shells help protect them from being crushed. Being self-protective makes people slow when they need to be fast, and awkward when they need to be nimble. In human terms, it's like protecting against fender benders by driving a tank: your vehicle won't get dented easily, but you won't get around very well (and you'll never get the thing to fit into a parking space). There's a better way.

We stop being fragile, said Taleb, by *growing* through instability, *thriving* in disorder, *loving* mistakes, and *enjoying* uncertainty. There is "no stability without volatility," he has written.[4] Andrew Zolli, a business innovator and social-change theorist, has called this attitude "resilience."[5] Resilient people spring back to their shape after distress. They don't avoid risk; they embrace it. Resilient people push forward when they're tempted to pull back.

Jesus didn't call his followers to avoid risk; he called them to be resilient. Among his last words before going to the cross was a prayer for his disciples: "I do not ask that you take them out of the world, but that you keep them from the evil one" (John 17:15).

It's not that resilient people live carelessly; it's that they don't let fear or regret bind them. The apostle Paul spent the first part of his life as a self-righteous bully and even an accessory to murder. Yet later on, he chose to set aside his regrets and run with abandon. He wrote, "Forgetting what lies behind and straining forward to what lies ahead, I press on toward the goal for the prize of the upward call of God in Christ Jesus" (Phil. 3:13–14). Nineteenth-century British preacher F. W. Robertson put it this way: "Victory is not obtained by the absence of mistakes. Forget mistakes. Retrieve victory from mistakes."[6]

Our mistakes don't *de*fine us; they *re*fine us. One of the best gifts we can give to those we love, and one of the most powerful weapons we can deploy against the evil one, is to set aside our past mistakes and live with endurance, for "endurance produces character, and character produces hope" (Rom. 5:4).

HOPE HELPS US LIVE CONFIDENTLY

If there is no God and this life is all there is, we have no choice but to orbit around ourselves. Our mistakes, shortcomings, and negative circumstances then form a perverse kind of gravity that fuses us to a molten core of desperation. But if we choose to orbit around the heart of the Father, who has removed our sins from us "as far as the east is from the west" (Ps. 103:12) and gives us "a future and a hope" (Jer. 29:11), then we are lifted away from the pull of our fears and regrets.

Even though I have been a Christian for a long time, it took a bout of depression for me to see the futility of orbiting around myself. My hopes dashed, I cried out, "God, you had better be there, because I have no place else to go!" Though my troubles were light compared with Job's, I began to sense what the man meant when he said, "Though he slay me, I will hope in him" (Job 13:15). I experienced a whole new orbit as I put my hope in God instead of myself (see Ps. 33:22). As Proverbs 23:18 says, "Surely there is a future, and your hope will not be cut off."

Love, healing, purpose, and peace all find their fulfillment in hope, and hope releases us from the most persistent of idea viruses: despair. Christians have had the privilege of bringing this good news to the world since the resurrection of Jesus. More than eighteen hundred years ago, an early writer described Christianity to a curious seeker this way: "What the soul is in the body, that are Christians in the world." Even the nonreligious have noticed. Jürgen Habermas is an atheist and Europe's most prominent public intellectual. He has said that the things humans love—such as equality and freedom—are the "the direct heir to the Judaic ethic of justice and the Christian ethic of love."[7] French philosopher (and atheist) Luc Ferry stated that because of its conviction that every person is made in God's image, it is to Christianity that Western civilization "owes its entire democratic inheritance."[8] Hope changes the world.

The virus of despair cannot destroy a body immunized by hope. So will hope ever be released from Pandora's jar?

INVEST IN YOURSELF AND OTHERS: FOUR THINGS YOU CAN DO RIGHT NOW TO RESTORE HOPE

In my imaginings, hope doesn't arrive in royal indifference. Rather, released from exile, she moves gracefully into our sickrooms, lifting the shades of despair, touching our fevered faces, willing us to be well. But hope doesn't leave us there. She pulls us out of bed, steadies us, and says, "Now go, rouse the others." Hope isn't just a rescuer; she's a recruiter. There are at least four ways we can be recruited to her side.

1. Face reality head on. Most people think they can have hope only when they ignore the realities of the world. To them, ignorance of what is going on is bliss. But to the Christian worldview, hope arrives in full view of what is real. There is much darkness in the world. Idea viruses infect people and even entire nations. A virus in the physical world can be stopped by identifying its characteristics, isolating its impact, informing people about how to stop it, and investing in the afflicted to help them recover. You have to pay close attention to reality to carry out each step. The same is true with idea viruses. Don't ignore reality; see it as God sees it.

2. Bring work gloves. Hope does not turn away. It gets busy. In a previous chapter, I mentioned how the city of my birth, Detroit, has languished for decades in crime and poverty. But today, hope rises in Detroit through ministries such as Grace Centers of Hope, which takes in the homeless, the drug addicted, and those being released from prison. The center gets its clients involved in caring churches, teaches them job skills, and helps them become homeowners. Of those who stick with the program at least four months, 87 percent finish and graduate sober.[9] Twelve thousand volunteers—including former addicts—make it happen.[10] In a world of despair, hope shows up in overalls, ready to work.

3. Choose to give life. As journalist Mindy Belz reflected on her years of visiting Iraqi and Syrian refugees, she said, "Destruction brought comfort, in the words of the prophet Nahum; impossible hardships became possible to endure, and death became life-giving."[11] In Iraq and Syria, even as ISIS tries to annihilate people and take over both countries, Christian relief workers are winning the battle for the hearts and minds of refugees by fearlessly bringing provisions and hope into insanely dangerous places. They carry out this life-giving task over the course of months and even years, returning again and again to war-torn areas. Hardship, "instead of ... moving their hands away from the fiery flame," Mindy witnessed, "moved them toward it—and toward one another."[12]

4. Don't put hope in yourself. A young man approached Jesus, asking what good deed he would have to perform to earn eternal life. Jesus told him that if he wanted treasure in heaven, he should sell what he possessed and give it to the poor. Scripture says the disheartened young man went away sorrowful, "for he had great possessions" (Mark 10:22). I squirm when I hear this story because I, too, have been guilty of putting my hope in what I think I possess, such as control of my time and money. This makes me fragile; I grow gloomy over being stuck in traffic or having to pay more for something than I think it is worth. When I don't feel in control, I assume that no one is in control. My problem is not that God is not God; it's that I suffer from unbelief.

Consider this contrast. On another occasion, a man whose little boy was tormented by an evil spirit approached Jesus. "If you can do anything, have compassion on us and help us," he said.

And Jesus said to him, "All things are possible for one who believes."

To which the father replied, crying out in desperation, "I believe; help my unbelief!" (Mark 9:22–24).

I love this father's honest expression of complete helplessness. He ached for his son and would do anything to help him get well. But he rightly sensed that his son's healing depended on God's power, not on whether he himself was capable of belief. Hope isn't about willing ourselves to believe something that isn't true; it's about trusting that God knows what he is doing. And what God is doing, pastor Timothy Keller has written, is "what you would have asked for if you knew everything he knows."[13] Seeing God for who he really is restores hope.

ONE MORE THING

Hope is being released even in the bleakest of circumstances as God's people trust him and refuse to give in. In her conversation with the Chaldean bishop of Aleppo, Antoine Audo, Mindy wondered why anyone with the ability to escape such a situation would remain. She summoned the courage to ask, "Will you stay?"

The bishop, who has seen two-thirds of Syrian Christians either killed or driven away, replied, "Of course. It's my country, the place I live, and I have to give a testimony. I respect everybody who chooses to leave. But I will continue."[14]

Moved by this description, I asked Mindy, "With everything you've seen, what keeps you from giving in to despair?" Mindy told me that the key thing she has learned from the persecuted church is that "they are willing to give up everything *except* their faith." In this, she said, "You often find an otherworldly kind of joy." I asked, "Do you think we might ever experience that kind of persecution here?" She replied that we might but added, "I think it will strip us of all the crutches other than faith, and then we see that not only our faith is real but it is a joy- and life-giving thing."[15]

Earlier I quoted Haldir the Elf from Tolkien's *The Fellowship of the Ring*, but I cut off the quote in the middle. After Haldir noted the evil in the world, he continued, "Still there is much that is fair, and though in all lands love is now mingled with grief, it grows perhaps the greater."[16]

This world can be dark. Standing for truth and fighting against evil and injustice seem to get us nowhere. Terror is real. Slavery and torture and death are real. But that is only half the story. Hope has been released and is recruiting others, one by one. Including me. Including you. This is why we can each declare freedom from idea viruses that threaten to steal our joy and seal our gloom: *There is hope for the world. I am not doomed. What is right and just and true will win.*

Which leaves us with one big question, put to me by an inquisitive yet skeptical student following a recent talk: "Let's assume that everything you say about God's existence and the reliability of the Bible is actually true. So what?" It took a personal crisis of faith for me to really grapple with it, and it might never have happened had not the battery on my MP3 player died in the middle of a run down a long country road.

CHAPTER 13

IS GOD EVEN RELEVANT?

How Jesus Conquers Idea Viruses Once and for All

"The question of God is simply irrelevant to so much of what we do on a daily basis that it eventually drops out of mind and heart," wrote theologian Craig M. Gay. "God is simply forgotten."[1] This describes my attitude as a young man. I didn't see God as relevant and couldn't wait to leave church as soon as I finished high school.

Had I been asked, I wouldn't have denied believing in God. But my theism was only theoretical. In practice, I was an atheist. I ignored biblical teachings that I found inconvenient. I based my actions on what felt good. I fled discomfort. I turned to God only for rescue from sticky situations.

Each day I was moving further from God in my decisions, values, and priorities. Thankfully, my parents intervened by arranging for me to travel to Colorado to take part in a program offered by Summit Ministries. Two weeks later, my course had begun to reverse, and not just because I learned intellectual arguments for God's existence. The leaders at Summit gave me new ways to think about the Christian faith. C. S. Lewis perfectly summarized what I came to embrace: "I believe in Christianity as I believe that the Sun has risen, not only because I see it, but because by it I see everything else."[2]

How we see the Christian faith shapes our view of the world, but how we understand God shapes it even more. Preacher and author A. W. Tozer said, "What comes into our minds when we think about God is the most important thing about us."[3] Before attending the Summit, very little came into my mind when I thought about God. At the Summit, I learned to see God as the *creator* through whom the universe came into being (see Gen. 1:1; John 1:1–3). I learned to see God as *sustainer* of the world, holding everything together (see Col. 1:17). I learned to see God as *communicator* to the world. The whole universe speaks the language of God,[4] and God is personally present in Jesus.

In time, my doubt faded. I knew that God is real, the Bible is true, and the Christian worldview makes sense. End of story. But when my world unexpectedly unraveled many years later, my doubt returned with a vengeance and I came *this close* to walking away from it all. Here's why I didn't.

WHEN EVERYTHING FELL APART

Having already worked out a Christian worldview to live by, in adulthood I pursued it with all my heart. Taking over the presidency of the Summit twenty-five years after attending as a student seemed like a natural fit. My wife and children were as excited as I was.

But then difficulties hit like a tidal wave. Helping students through life crises wore me out emotionally. A wildfire forced the evacuation of our facilities for several weeks. Financial struggles plagued the ministry. That fall, my children found it hard to adjust in their schooling. And in a tragic set of circumstances, my wife sustained a brain injury in a cycling accident, recovered, and then chose to end our marriage. Counseling was to no avail.

Initially, as my life seemed to come apart, I found myself drawing closer to God in worship, prayer, and service. I worked hard to be a good dad. Friends told me they admired how I was handling things. Yet the stress was constant. My children were angry. The pain inside continued to grow.

My pastor was concerned. "How are you doing with God?" he asked. "Are you upset with him?"

"Not really," I answered. It was true. If anything, my intellectual faith in God's existence and goodness had grown as I put the finishing touches on three worldview books—each one running five or six hundred pages—that explain the reasons behind the Christian faith.[5] But emotionally, I just felt numb.

Time did not heal this numbness. Some of my buddies, alarmed by my fading hope, invited me to reboot through a week-long hunting trip. The second day, we bagged our limit by noon and most of the guys settled in for naps. Unable to rest, I set out for a long run.

Jogging along country roads that surrounded the hunting lodge, I suddenly felt overcome by sadness. Turning up the music on my MP3 player kept my mind off the growing discomfort. But then the battery died. All was silent except the crunch of gravel beneath my feet. There is no more profound sense of isolation than being alone with comfortless thoughts.

That's when I broke. Quivering, I felt tears spilling down my face as suppressed emotions rushed to the surface. I tried praying, but the only words that came out were "God, what did I do to deserve this? I have *loved* you. I have *served* you. *What more do you want from me?*"

I felt guilty accusing God, but remorse quickly gave way to fresh anger. Racking sobs came out in gasps. "I'll tell you what you are," I said to God. "*You* are a *bully*."

For two hours I ran, lecturing God, pleading with him for relief, apologizing for my lack of faith, and then bursting out in defiant curses once again. Finally, utterly spent, I made my way back to the lodge, showered, and fell into a deep sleep. I hoped I would never have to wake.

It was one of the bleakest days of my life. But strangely, it also was a turning point. The pain inside alerted me to idea viruses lodged in my heart and mind that convinced me that I was unloved, that I was a failure, and that there was no hope for guys like me.

In the end, I found rescue in the place I least expected: my childhood faith in Jesus. Returning to that began to restore the love, healing, purpose, peace, and hope I had craved.

The Secret Battle of Ideas about God describes my struggle with idea viruses. I would not be surprised if it describes yours too. Maybe you've sought love but settled for lust. Maybe you've desired healing but settled for numbness. Maybe you've craved meaning but settled for busyness. Maybe you've wished for peace but settled for icy silence. Maybe you've prayed for hope but settled for distraction.

My journey has taught me this: the gospel isn't just good news for those who have never heard; it's good news for those who love Jesus but wrestle with what this means in everyday life.

LIVING AS IF JESUS'S PROMISES ARE TRUE

In *The Secret Battle of Ideas about God*, we've examined five fatal worldviews that promise answers to life's deepest questions but in fact only multiply our misery. In turn, we've seen how Jesus enables each believer in him to declare five things to be true.

"I AM LOVED"

Deep, unconditional love exists, and I can have it. Of the three most frequently used Greek words for love, *philos*, love of family, explains the sort of love that compels us to promote our offspring's survival. *Eros*, sexual love, explains why we are compelled to reproduce. But these loves are incomplete without God's love, *agape*, a selfless, humble, gentle, cheerful, hopeful, burden-bearing, self-giving, enduring love. *Agape* harmonizes all other loves. It is the kind of love that never goes away.

Because believers have received agape (see Rom. 5:5), they can offer it to others. When I'm frustrated with a delayed flight, agape enables me to see the airline employee as a person Jesus loves and not just an obstacle preventing me from reaching my destination. Similarly, the homeless man on the corner may seem lazy or weak willed to me, but agape spotlights his loveliness because of Jesus's kind of love.

"MY SUFFERING WILL BE OVERCOME"

Hurt will not win. Indeed, it already has lost. Jesus told his followers that he had overcome the world's troubles (see John 16:33). He had secured *nikao*, or victory, depriving evil of its ability to harm us forever. When I'm mistreated, I remember that one day Jesus will wipe every tear from my eyes (see Rev. 21:4). When I am afraid, Jesus offers a peace that is not of this world (see John 14:27). When I observe others who are suffering from the effects of an unhealthy upbringing or their poor choices or an addiction, I can walk alongside without having to fix them, trusting God for victory.

Other worldviews fall short in helping us find healing. They say we ought to just dampen the pain or wait for a revolution or resign ourselves to meaninglessness. Jesus rises above these views. Pain isn't a sign that Jesus has lost the victory; it's a reminder that we haven't yet experienced the full extent of his triumph.

"I HAVE AN INCREDIBLE CALLING"

My life has meaning. I bear God's image, and he has called me. The word *call* is related to the Greek word *kaleo*, "to summon." The

One who knows all things calls me to restored meaning. When my job is frustrating, I know I'm there for a purpose. When parenting isn't going my way, I can remember that it, too, is a holy calling. Nothing—*nothing*—happens by meaningless chance.

Life takes on meaning when I see it from God's viewpoint. Gazing at the heavens from a purely human perspective, the late astronomer Carl Sagan said, "The Cosmos is all that is or ever was or ever will be."[6] Gazing at the heavens from God's perspective, though, King David marveled at God's awesome work and the special place he has given to humanity (see Ps. 8:3–5). Carl Sagan and King David both viewed the same stars, the same planets, the same galaxies. Yet Sagan, a God denier, saw his own significance in light of his smallness. David, a God embracer, saw his own significance in light of God's bigness. Because of God, we are not lost in the cosmos. Our lives have meaning.

"I AM MEANT FOR COMMUNITY"

I can overcome conflict and live at peace with those around me. The Christian worldview says conflict is both "in here" and "out there," caused by sin, which breaks our relationships with God and with others. Healing begins with shalom, a vision of a peacefully content life in which our needs are met as we meet the needs of others. What is broken becomes unbroken.

Shalom doesn't just hold things together until we're rescued from this planet; it places us smack-dab in the middle of real life, where decayed things need repairing, evil needs opposing, and ugly things need beautifying. Based on shalom, I'm learning to not ignore conflict but press into it by seeing the person with whom I am in tension as an image bearer of God. I'm learning to ask questions instead of making accusations. When a social-media post irks me, I search for a response that doesn't pour fuel on the flames. I can't control what other people do, but as it depends on me, I can live at peace with all (see Rom. 12:18).

"THERE IS HOPE FOR THE WORLD"

I am not doomed. What is right and just and true will win. To those embracing fatal worldviews, though, hope seems far off because they think nothing will change unless everything changes. Meanwhile, life is nothing more than an "episode between two oblivions," as the American philosopher Ernest Nagel glumly asserted.[7]

From a Christian worldview, hope is real and we can have it. The same word used for hope in the myth of Pandora, *elpis*, also is used in the Scriptures to express the hope we can have in Jesus. Finding my hope in Jesus has changed my viewpoint in surprising ways. I'm often called on to take a stand on social issues. I know I'll be criticized no matter what I say. So with hope, I move forward, fearless because God is with me (see Isa. 41:10). When I'm discouraged, I can remember that I live in a world in which Jesus has risen from the dead (see Phil. 3:10). No power on earth can change that. Confident hope is ours through Jesus (see Rom. 12:12 NLT).

These five declarations changed everything for me just when I thought I might give in to despair. They also helped me see that I had overlooked something important about knowing God, something that has opened a whole new chapter in my life.

TWO WAYS WE EACH NEED TO KNOW GOD

It is true that idea viruses have the world spinning out of control. Every worldview offers a way of salvation. But if what we've seen about the Christian worldview is true, they can't save us in the way we need to be saved. The Christian worldview says the answer is to be reconciled to God.

Most believers think there is only one kind of reconciliation with God, which is trusting Jesus as their savior. But that is only part of the story. If we want to escape the idea viruses that keep us from the things we desire most in life, we need to understand two things, not just one.

1. RECONCILIATION IS A JOURNEY *TO* GOD

The first part of getting right with God is to stop going our own way. We are to repent. The New Testament word for "repentance" is *metanoia*, which means "changing one's way of life." In ancient times, *metanoia* meant leaving behind an inferior way of life and pursuing an enlightened path. The New Testament of the Bible says Jesus is *the* way to God (see John 14:6). John says it is through Jesus that God has made his dwelling among us (see 1:14).

Jesus isn't just a special person who makes God seem friendlier; he is the Messiah, the one an ancient prophecy said would be named Immanuel, "God is with us" (see Isa. 7:14; Matt. 1:23). It's not merely that God was with us in the past or that he will come back in the future. God is with us right now in Jesus. The Bible presents humans as criminals whose sin establishes their guilt beyond a shadow of a doubt. Yet the criminals are offered, through Jesus, complete pardon by the Judge of the universe.

You don't have to be good enough. Change comes through Christ's sacrifice, not before it. Paul wrote, "God shows his love for us in that while we were still sinners, Christ died for us" (Rom. 5:8). Nor do you have to be capable. God does it, "for it is God who works in you, both to will and to work for his good pleasure" (Phil. 2:13).

That's the gospel. The good news. Some think the gospel ends with God's "not guilty" verdict. What more is there to do except leave the courtroom and go on with your life? But if what the Bible says about God is true, then we walk out of God's courtroom by his side in a journey that touches every aspect of creation.

2. RECONCILIATION IS A JOURNEY *WITH* GOD

In trusting Jesus, we come to *know* God so we can *love* him. In the journey itself, though, it's the other way around: we *love* him in order to *know* him. If you've ever fallen in love, you know what it means to feel, "I want to know everything there is to know about this person!" Love for God makes us want to enter into his mystery, to truly know him.

Christians make an enormous mistake when they forget that God is in charge of everything. There is no division between the sacred part of life—the life of worship—and the secular part of life, things such as work and art and public policy. According to professor Nancy Pearcey, if we could see the connection, we could see the gospel liberated to reach the entire culture.[8]

Every day at the Summit, we see students liberated from idea viruses and prepared to bring Jesus's transformation to culture. Take Bek, for example. At one time, she had trusted God with everything. Over the years, though, she found herself struggling. Daily anxiety attacks incapacitated her, and anxiety escalated into hopelessness. "Not a day went by without my considering ending my life," she said. Finally, she told God, "I'm so done. You're not there for me when I need you most."

At the Summit, Bek experienced the selfless love of the staff. Two mentors in particular, Caroline and Sam, cared for her without reservation, even though she was bitter toward God and others. As she listened to lectures from world-class theologians and philosophers, Bek began regaining confidence that God is real, loves her, and has a plan for her and for the world.

One day Sam asked Bek what was holding her back from giving herself to God. She spilled out her fears, regrets, and bitterness. Caroline joined them for prayer, and Bek committed her life to Jesus. "I have never been more scared in my life," said

Bek, "but their unconditional love encouraged me to overcome what I had been facing."

Love, healing, meaning, peace, and hope came together for Bek, like the five points of a star. In feeling loved, she was able to open her heart to God's healing. In turn, this gave her the inner peace she craved and restored her relationship with her family. Now she lives with hope.

Austin came to study at the Summit just to please his family. Everything about him screamed, *I don't want to be here!* Before coming, he had sarcastically joked with his friends, "God is going to be in Colorado, and I'm going to find him there," meaning, of course, that no such thing would happen.

At the Summit, Austin's mentor met with him one on one, engaging him with questions and listening without judgment. The mentor noticed that as Austin began feeling safe, there was a visible change in his attitude, body language, and overall demeanor. Listening carefully to lectures about the truth of Scripture, Austin concluded, "The Bible is true; that stuff actually happened."

Austin believed the evidence, but he needed to make a decision without being forced. On the last evening, I asked him, "What barriers stop you from living fully for Jesus?" Later that night, Austin prayed with his mentor, who commented that Austin's prayer was "one of the most genuine prayers I've ever heard: from the heart and not fluffed up by Christian jargon."

We can see all four steps to stopping viruses—identify, isolate, inform, and invest—at work in both Bek's and Austin's stories. Here's what it means to each of us.

PREPARING OURSELVES AND HELPING PREPARE OTHERS

Bek and Austin will have ups and downs in their lives, as we all do. But their stories, while exciting, are not unique. Christians are being rescued from idea viruses all the time, and the clarity of truth comes to them in just the way we've seen in previous chapters.

IDENTIFY

In my writing, work, and various ministry involvements, I spend a lot of time identifying the idea viruses that spring from counterfeit worldviews such as secularism, Marxism, postmodernism, new spirituality, and Islam. Over the years, I have benefited from the insight of Summit's extensive network of instructors and advisors who help Christians respond biblically to cultural challenges. I put that wisdom to work in my own life and as I help others. I trust that as you have read this book, you have found ways to strengthen your resistance to idea viruses, as well as ways you can help others as the battle of ideas continues to rage.

ISOLATE

After identifying the counterfeit worldviews that compete for our loyalty, we isolate the likely impact of idea viruses so we can help Christians see how they are affected personally. For example, if we wonder whether we are loved, it's important to see the ways in which culture separates sex from love. In working through this process, we can isolate the counterfeit idea that we are solely sexual, and not spiritual, beings. Or when we hear the constant refrain that the rich are not paying their fair share, we can learn to see how easily a spirit of resentment can develop that discourages us from bringing our own entrepreneurial ideas to life. Christian experts in various fields can do much to help us isolate idea viruses such as these.

INFORM

I recommend that you seek out biblical teachers of apologetics, worldviews, economics, ethics, marriage and family, and other issues. The input you receive from people who have invested years developing their expertise can build your confidence in defending a Christian worldview. It also helps you pass on this important knowledge to others in a compelling, compassionate way. We all need to learn how to give an answer for our faith (see 1 Pet. 3:15). The teachers I work with don't just offer facts; they share their life stories, and they listen.

INVEST

We want people to feel safe and cared for so they can knock down the barriers that would stop them from living fully for Jesus. Forever. Everyone on our team at the Summit, from maintenance workers to vice presidents, is trained in a Christian worldview and prepared to engage others in discussion. We strive to create an environment in which the Holy Spirit can work in people's lives, guiding them to the truth.

This process intertwines truth and relationship like two strands of a DNA double helix, allowing students to begin developing healthy spiritual DNA in their lives to replace the distorted genetic code fed to them by idea viruses. It's not a onetime act; it's an everyday, all-of-life process.

HERE WE ARE AT THE BEGINNING

In chapter 1, I shared the story of Rick Rescorla, a hero of 9/11 who saved thousands of lives by instinctively living out his worldview. Rick declared what he believed: that he would stay tough when facing the enemy and leave no one behind. As he guided people to safety after the attack on the World Trade Center, he sang this declaration through his bullhorn: "Men of Cornwall, stand ye steady. Stand and never yield!"

In the secret battle of ideas, we've declared five things to be true: we are loved, evil will not win, our lives have purpose, we can be creators of peace, and we have hope for the future. These declarations confront the stealth attacks of idea viruses. But these declarations are mere shadows of a coming reality. Revelation 5:9–13 says that at the end of all things, the redeemed will sing a new song to Jesus, the one who made every good thing possible: "To him who sits on the throne and to the Lamb be blessing and honor and glory and might forever and ever!"

Because of Jesus, fear and despair cannot destroy us. His love is unconditional. His victory is unconquerable. His purpose is unassailable. His peace is unbreakable. His hope is undeniable. Yes, we are in a secret battle of ideas, but the outcome is assured. Jesus has won.

ACKNOWLEDGMENTS

I wrote this book all by myself and it flowed so easily that I didn't even need help from others.

Uh, not. *Absolutely* not.

This was the hardest writing I've endeavored. It would never have come together if not for an extraordinary team effort.

Tosha Payne kept Summit Ministries' executive office together during the countless hours I struggled to write. As my editor, Ron Lee guided me away from clanging philosopher-speak to sound a clear, warm note in my writing. Karl Schaller, with *The Secret Battle of Ideas about God* vision clearly in mind, managed a lengthy project punch list and coached me toward writing excellence. He was ably assisted by Amanda Bridger, who eats complicated details for lunch, and by Aaron Klemm, who is managing and marketing *The Secret Battle of Ideas about God* product line with infectious enthusiasm.

Jeff Wood essentially ran Summit while I wrote and worked through the trials discussed in these pages. Other members of

Summit's leadership team, Aaron Atwood and Eric Smith, pastored me and interceded for me. Every man should have such a band of brothers.

Lots of people listened patiently as I read chapters aloud. These long-sufferers include Stephanie Large, Roy and Jackie Myers, Graham Myers, Summit staff (during staff chapels, no less), Summit Semester students, and Lumerit Scholars at the capstone course in Estes Park.

I love the whimsical yet powerful video Andrew Winchell and Luke Riley put together to accompany this book. David Kinnaman and the Barna Group have helped give this project very long legs. At David C Cook, Abby DeBenedittis and Cara Iverson proved to be wonderfully thorough editors, and Verne Kenney, Tim Peterson, and Chriscynethia Floyd have never wavered as champions of *The Secret Battle of Ideas about God*.

Thank you to our faithful Summit faculty members, John Stonestreet, in particular, for the countless hours of feedback, ideas, and suggestions, and for the wonderful interviews.

Sid and Carol Verdoorn, Alex and Jan Floyd, Steve and Nelly Greisen, and the staff of the Bodleian Library at Oxford provided "undisclosed locations" from which I could reflect, write, and edit.

Each person who touched this project has been an agent of mercy, demonstrating God's faithfulness. It is to them and to the extended Summit family of students, supporters, and friends that I dedicate this book.

The steadfast love of the LORD never ceases;
his mercies never come to an end;
they are new every morning;
great is your faithfulness.
(Lam. 3:22–23)

NOTES

FOREWORD

1. George Barna, *Think Like Jesus: Make the Right Decision Every Time* (Brentwood, TN: Integrity Publishers, 2003), 6.

2. David Kinnaman and Gabe Lyons, *Good Faith: Being a Christian When Society Thinks You're Irrelevant and Extreme* (Grand Rapids, MI: Baker, 2016), 58.

CHAPTER 1: INVISIBLE WARFARE

1. Michael Grunwald, "A Tower of Courage," *Washington Post*, October 28, 2001, www.washingtonpost.com/archive/lifestyle/2001/10/28/a-tower-of-courage /c53e8244-3754-440f-84f8-51f841aff6c8/?utm_term=.87a8eb84810a.

2. Atheist author Richard Dawkins has written extensively about what he calls "mind viruses," a metaphor that is closely related to his concept of the meme, a word he coined in his book *The Selfish Gene* (Oxford: Oxford University Press, 1976, 2016). For more on these concepts, see Mark Jordan, "What's in a Meme?," Richard Dawkins Foundation for Reason & Science, February 4, 2014, https://richarddawkins.net/2014/02/whats-in-a-meme/.

3. Aristotle, *Nicomachean Ethics*, trans. C. D. C. Reeve (Indianapolis: Hackett, 2014), 21.

4. Rick Rescorla, "Lt. Rick Rescorla, B Company, 2nd Battalion, 7th Calvary Air Mobile," YouTube video, 8:02, "The Voice of the Prophet" interview on July 28, 1998, posted by "CVL23USSPRINCETON," November 20, 2011, www.youtube.com/watch?v=vGXjjgMLQVs.

5. James B. Stewart, "The Real Heroes Are Dead: A Love Story," *New Yorker*, February 11, 2002, www.newyorker.com/magazine/2002/02/11/the-real -heroes-are-dead.

6. H. G. Moore and Joseph L. Galloway, *We Were Soldiers Once ... and Young: Ia Drang—The Battle That Changed the War in Vietnam* (New York: Presidio, 2004), 201.

7. Stewart, "Real Heroes."

8. Stewart, "Real Heroes."

9. Grunwald, "Tower of Courage."

CHAPTER 2: STOPPING BAD IDEAS

1. Ebola-Zaire is named after the Ebola River in the country that was called Zaire until a 1997 coup overthrew its dictator, Mobutu Sese Seko. The country is now named the Democratic Republic of Congo. The Ebola-Zaire virus killed nine out of ten of those infected during a 1976 outbreak.

2. Since 1940, researchers had identified nearly 250 viruses that had leaped from animals to humans; see Alok Jha, "A Deadly Disease Could Travel at Jet Speed around the World. How Do We Stop It in Time?," *Guardian*, November 12, 2013, www.theguardian.com/science/2013/nov/12/deadly -disease-modern-global-epidemic. For example, the mosquito-borne Zika virus jumped from rhesus monkeys to humans; see Edward B. Hayes, "Zika Virus outside Africa," *Emerging Infectious Diseases* 15, no. 9 (2009): 1347–50, www.ncbi.nlm.nih.gov/pmc/articles/PMC2819875/.

3. "The Deadly Virus: The Influenza Epidemic of 1918," National Archives and Records Administration, www.archives.gov/exhibits/influenza-epidemic/.

4. "Deadly Virus."

5. Richard Preston, "Crisis in the Hot Zone," *New Yorker*, October 26, 1992, 62.

6. "Outbreak of Swine-Origin Influenza A (H1N1) Virus Infection—Mexico, March–April 2009," MMWR, April 30, 2009, www.cdc.gov/mmwr /preview/mmwrhtml/mm58d0430a2.htm; Daniel Nasaw et al., "Europeans Urged to Avoid Mexico and US as Swine Flu Death Toll Rises," *Guardian*, April 27, 2009, www.theguardian.com/world/2009 /apr/27/swine-flu-mexico.

7. R. J. Rummel demonstrated that more human beings in the twentieth century died at the hands of their governments committed to Marxist

or fascist ideology than in all previous centuries combined. See *Death by Government* (New Brunswick, NJ: Transaction, 1994).

8. Rob Fowler, "Fighting Ebola from Day One," World Health Organization, January 2015, www.who.int/features/2015/ebola-interview-fowler/en/.

9. "2014 Ebola Outbreak in West Africa: Case Counts," Centers for Disease Control and Prevention, April 13, 2016, www.cdc.gov/vhf/ebola /outbreaks/2014-west-africa/case-counts.html.

10. Alok Jha, "A Deadly Disease Could Travel at Jet Speed around the World. How Do We Stop It in Time?," *The Guardian*, November 12, 2013, www.theguardian.com/science/2013/nov/12/deadly-disease-modern -global-epidemic.

11. This analogy comes from Richard Preston's stunning article "Crisis in the Hot Zone" (*New Yorker*, October 26, 1992), which led to the writing of a bestselling book and introduced the world to the Ebola crisis back in 1992. Preston describes in simple language how viruses like the Marburg virus and Ebola work.

12. "An Infinity of Viruses," National Geographic, "Phenomena," February 20, 2013, http://phenomena.nationalgeographic.com/2013/02/20/an-infinity -of-viruses/.

13. Michaeleen Doucleff, "How Ebola Kills You: It's Not the Virus," NPR, August 26, 2014, www.npr.org/sections/goatsandsoda/2014/08/26 /342451672/how-ebola-kills-you-its-not-the-virus.

14. For the purposes of this book, I've taken the liberty to restate the way Dr. Fowler and other medical professionals talk about these four steps. Here are the four terms Fowler uses: epidemiology, contact tracing, social mobilization, and infection prevention and control; see Rob Fowler, "Fighting Ebola from Day One," World Health Organization, January 2015, www.who.int/features/2015/ebola-interview-fowler/en/.

15. Admittedly, clear statistics are hard to come by. Here are some sources you can check out. Christian Smith, author of *Soul Searching: The Religious and Spiritual Lives of American Teenagers* (New York: Oxford University Press, 2005), believes that what passes for Christianity among young adults who grew up in the church is often actually "moralistic therapeutic deism," a term that has come to describe the way young adults believe that if they are good, God will love them and give them what they want. Gary Railsback's research is more well grounded but older. He found that between 30 and 50 percent of young adults who claim to be born-again Christians as college freshmen claim not to be born-again Christians when they graduate;

see "Faith Commitment of Born-Again Students at Secular and Evangelical Colleges," *Journal of Research on Christian Education* 15, no. 1 (2006): 39–60. In addition, Scott McConnell reported that 75 percent of students who were significantly involved in church in high school are no longer even attending church as twentysomethings in "LifeWay Research Finds Reasons 18- to 22-Year-Olds Drop Out of Church," LifeWay Articles, www.lifeway.com/Article/LifeWay-Research-finds-reasons-18-to-22-year -olds-drop-out-of-church.

16. Mark D. Regnerus and Jeremy E. Uecker, "How Corrosive Is College to Religious Faith and Practice?," Social Science Research Council, February 5, 2007, http://religion.ssrc.org/reforum/Regnerus_Uecker.pdf.

17. For biblical passages about working and sharing, see Psalm 112:9; Isaiah 58:7; 2 Corinthians 8:14; Ephesians 4:28; 1 Timothy 6:18; Hebrews 13:16; 1 Peter 4:9. As opposed to these passages, Marxism demands that wealth be redistributed by force and that private property be abolished.

18. There are many differences among religions such as Buddhism, Hinduism, Taoism, Shintoism, and Confucianism (and Western religions such as new age thought, Wicca, neo-paganism, and scientology), so grouping them together seems a little unfair. But each view is pantheistic, which comes from two Greek words, *pan*, which means "all," and *theos*, which means "god." All is god. Everything that exists is one thing.

19. For a thorough, documented approach to these six worldviews, see Jeff Myers and David A. Noebel, *Understanding the Times: A Survey of Competing Worldviews* (Colorado Springs, CO: David C Cook, 2015).

20. See, for example, William J. McGuire and Demetrios Papageorgis, "The Relative Efficacy of Various Types of Prior Belief-Defense in Producing Immunity against Persuasion," *Journal of Abnormal and Social Psychology* 62, (1961): 327–37.

21. Em Griffin, *The Mind Changers: The Art of Christian Persuasion* (Wheaton, IL: Tyndale, 1976), 172–76.

22. Robert A. Fowler et al., "Caring for Critically Ill Patients with Ebola Virus Disease: Perspectives from West Africa," *American Journal of Respiratory and Critical Care Medicine* 190, no. 7 (October 2014): 733–37, www.atsjournals.org/doi/pdf/10.1164/rccm.201408-1514CP; T. E. West and A. von Saint André-von Arnim, "Clinical Presentation and Management of Severe Ebola Virus Disease," *Annals of the*

American Thoracic Society 11, no. 9 (November 2014): 1341–50, www.ncbi.nlm.nih.gov/pubmed/25369317.

23. John R. W. Stott, *Basic Christianity* (Grand Rapids, MI: Eerdmans, 1971), 21.

CHAPTER 3: AM I LOVED?

1. Rukmini Callimachi, "ISIS and the Lonely Young American," *New York Times*, June 27, 2015, www.nytimes.com/2015/06/28/world/americas /isis-online-recruiting-american.html.

2. Nasser Weddady, quoted in Callimachi, "ISIS and the Lonely Young American."

3. Mubin Shaikh, quoted in Callimachi, "ISIS and the Lonely Young American."

4. Jon Hamilton, "Orphans' Lonely Beginnings Reveal How Parents Shape a Child's Brain," NPR, February 24, 2014, www.npr.org/sections/health-shots /2014/02/20/280237833/orphans-lonely-beginnings-reveal-how-parents -shape-a-childs-brain.

5. Karl Marx, "The Fetishism of Commodities and the Secret Thereof," in *Capital: A Critique of Political Economy*, ed. Frederick Engels, trans. Samuel Moore and Edward Aveling (Moscow: Progress, 1970), www.marxists.org/archive /marx/works/1867-c1/ch01.htm#S4.

6. Frederick Engels, *The Origin of the Family, Private Property and the State* (New York: International Publishers, 1942), 67.

7. Glenn Ward, *Teach Yourself Postmodernism*, 2nd ed. (Chicago: McGraw-Hill, 2003), 146.

8. Foucault even declared himself a disciple of the Marquis de Sade. The Marquis de Sade was a French aristocrat who sexually mistreated everyone around him and gleefully recorded his violent and criminal acts in books. The term *sadism*, the enjoyment of inflicting pain on others, is derived from his name. See Mark Lilla, *The Reckless Mind: Intellectuals in Politics* (New York: New York Review Books, 2001), 142, for more on the Marquis de Sade.

9. Michel Foucault, paraphrased in Ward, *Teach Yourself Postmodernism*, 146.

10. *Washington Times*, August 31, 1997, B2.

11. Marianne Williamson, *A Return to Love: Reflections on the Principles of "A Course in Miracles"* (New York: HarperPerennial, 1996), 81.

12. Arielle Ford, "Manifest the Relationship of Your Dreams," The Chopra Center, www.chopra.com/ccl/manifest-the-relationship-of-your-dreams.

13. Sexuality, lamented conservative commentator Rod Dreher, "is how the modern American claims his freedom." "Sex after Christianity: Gay Marriage Is Not Just a Social Revolution but a Cosmological One," *The American Conservative*, April 11, 2013, www.theamericanconservative.com/articles/sex -after-christianity/.

14. C. S. Lewis calls a lie the idea that "any sexual act to which you are tempted at the moment is also healthy and normal." *Mere Christianity* (New York: HarperOne, 2001), 100.

15. Rollo May, *Psychology and the Human Dilemma* (New York: W. W. Norton, 1996), 188.

16. Kurt Conklin, "Adolescent Sexual Behavior: Demographics," Advocates for Youth, February 2012, www.advocatesforyouth.org/publications /publications-a-z/413-adolescent-sexual-behavior-i-demographics.

17. "American College Health Association–National College Health Assessment II: Spring 2015 Reference Group Executive Summary," American College Health Association, 2015, www.acha-ncha.org/docs/NCHA-II_WEB_SPRING _2015_REFERENCE_GROUP_EXECUTIVE_SUMMARY.pdf.

18. Ray Bohlin, "The Epidemic of Sexually Transmitted Diseases," LeaderU.com, 1993, www.leaderu.com/orgs/probe/docs/epid-std.html.

19. For these and other statistics, see Meg Meeker, *Epidemic: How Teen Sex Is Killing Our Kids* (Washington, DC: LifeLine, 2002).

20. "HIV among Youth," Centers for Disease Control and Prevention, April 27, 2016, www.cdc.gov/hiv/group/age/youth/.

21. Sophia Lee, "Recycling a Tragedy," *World*, October 3, 2015, 47, 50.

22. Those who have engaged in premarital sex fairly often are more likely to be unfaithful after marriage; see Andrew Greeley, *Faithful Attraction: Discovering Intimacy, Love, and Fidelity in American Marriage* (New York: Tom Doherty Associates, 1991), 201. Woman who are sexually active prior to marriage face a considerably higher risk of marital disruption; see Joan R. Kahn and Kathryn A. London, "Premarital Sex and the Risk of Divorce," *Journal of Marriage and Family* 53, no. 4 (1991): 845–55. Sexually active girls are more than three times as likely to report depressive symptoms as those who abstain, and sexually active boys are more than twice as likely to report depressive symptoms. In fact, these two groups report a higher incidence of suicide attempts; boys in particular are at eight times the risk for a suicide attempt if they are sexually active; see Robert E. Rector, Kirk A. Johnson,

and Lauren R. Noyes, "Sexually Active Teenagers Are More Likely to Be Depressed and to Attempt Suicide," Heritage Foundation, June 3, 2003, www.heritage.org/education/report/sexually-active-teenagers-are-more-likely-be-depressed-and-attempt-suicide.

23. Doug Eshleman, "Men View Half-Naked Women as Objects, Study Finds," *Daily Princetonian*, February 17, 2009, www.dailyprincetonian.com/article /2009/02/men-view-half-naked-women-as-objects-study-finds.

24. William Struthers, quoted in Janice Shaw Crouse, *Marriage Matters: Perspectives on the Private and Public Importance of Marriage* (New Brunswick, NJ: Transaction, 2012), 71.

25. See this statistic and many other statistics about pornography at "Pornography Statistics," Family Safe Media, accessed March 27, 2015, http://familysafemedia.com/pornography_statistics.html.

26. "Study: Rising Number of Kids Exposed to Online Porn," *Fox News*, February 5, 2007, www.foxnews.com/story/2007/02/05/study-rising -number-kids-exposed-to-online-porn.html.

27. April Reese Sorrow, "Magazine Trends Study Finds Increase in Advertisements Using Sex," *UGA Today*, June 5, 2012, http://news.uga.edu /releases/article/magazine-trends-study-finds-increase-in-advertisements -using-sex/.

28. Take same-sex marriage, for example. Sociologist Mark Regnerus said that "of the men who view pornographic material 'every day or almost every day,' 54 percent 'strongly agreed' that gay and lesbian marriage should be legal, compared with around 13 percent of those whose porn-use patterns were either monthly or less often than that." In this study, porn use emerged as a significant variable when a person's political views, marital status, age, religion, and even sexual orientation were taken into account. See "Porn Use and Supporting Same-Sex Marriage," *Public Discourse*, December 20, 2012, www.thepublicdiscourse.com/2012/12/7048/. Apparently, other researchers have speculated that pornography use "acti- vates a sexually 'liberal' mind-set" that "embraces non-judgment toward and even approval of nontraditional sexual behavior." Paul J. Wright and Ashley K. Randall, "Pornography Consumption, Education, and Support for Same-Sex Marriage among Adult U.S. Males," *Communication Research* 41, no. 5 (July 2014): 665–89.

29. William Shakespeare, *Romeo and Juliet* (Oxford: Oxford University Press, 2000), 157.

30. Douglas Coupland, *Life after God* (New York: Pocket Books, 1995), 359.

CHAPTER 4: LOVE NEVER FAILS

1. Linda White, "Texas Needs Alternatives to Prison Terms for Kids," *Chron*, June 19, 2013, www.chron.com/opinion/outlook/article/White-Texas -needs-alternatives-to-prison-terms-4610470.php.

2. Naveena Kottoor, "How Do People Forgive a Crime like Murder?," *BBC News*, August 20, 2013, www.bbc.com/news/magazine-23716713/.

3. White, "Texas Needs Alternatives."

4. Mark Obbie, "He Killed Her Daughter. She Forgave Him," *Slate*, June 30, 2015, www.slate.com/articles/news_and_politics/crime/2015/06/gary _brown_and_linda_white_he_killed_her_daughter_she_found_a_way_to _forgive.html.

5. Linda L. White, "Forgiving My Daughter's Killer," OnFaith, June 11, 2010, www.faithstreet.com/onfaith/2010/06/11/forgiving-my-daughters-killer /8019.

6. White, "Texas Needs Alternatives."

7. Paul J. Achtemeier, ed., *Harper's Bible Dictionary* (San Francisco: Harper and Row, 1985), 14.

8. Bruce Marshall, *The World, the Flesh, and Father Smith* (Boston: Houghton Mifflin, 1945), 108.

9. Kathleen Elkins, "The Way Billionaire Warren Buffett Defines Success Has Nothing to Do with Money," *Business Insider*, September 25, 2015, www.businessinsider.com/warren-buffett-defines-success-with-love-2015-9. Buffett went on to encourage students to give love away because that way they'll get more.

10. Monika Ardelt, "Effects of Religion and Purpose in Life on Elders' Subjective Well-Being and Attitudes toward Death," *Journal of Religious Gerontology* 14, no. 4 (2003): 57.

11. Keith A. King et al., "Increasing Self-Esteem and School Connectedness through a Multidimensional Mentoring Program," *Journal of School Health* 72, no. 7 (September 2002): 294; see also Rachel C. Vreeman and Aaron E. Carroll, "A Systematic Review of School-Based Interventions to Prevent Bullying," *Archives of Pediatric and Adolescent Medicine* 161, no. 1 (January 2007): 86.

12. Bonnie Bernard, "Resiliency: What We Have Learned," WestEd, 2004, www.wested.org/online_pubs/resiliency/resiliency.40pg.pdf, 8.

13. Jean M. Twenge and W. Keith Campbell, *The Narcissism Epidemic: Living in the Age of Entitlement* (New York: Atria, 2009), 2.

14. These and more examples may be found in Paul Johnson, *Intellectuals: From Marx and Tolstoy to Sartre and Chomsky* (New York: Harper and Row, 1988).

15. Dale S. Kuehne, *Sex and the iWorld: Rethinking Relationship beyond an Age of Individualism* (Grand Rapids, MI: Baker Academic, 2009), 143.

16. As Saint Augustine put it, "Temperance is love keeping itself entire and incorrupt for God; fortitude is love bearing everything readily for the sake of God; justice is love, serving God only, and therefore ruling well all else, as subject to man; prudence is love making a right distinction between what helps it toward God and what might hinder it." Quoted in H. Richard Niebuhr, *Christ and Culture* (New York: Harper and Brothers, 1951), 214.

17. Christian Smith, quoted in John Piippo, "(Christian Smith on) What Is a Person?," John Piippo, July 11, 2011, www.johnpiippo.com/2011/07 /christian-smith-on-what-is-person.html.

18. Armand M. Nicholi Jr., *The Question of God: C. S. Lewis and Sigmund Freud Debate God, Love, Sex, and the Meaning of Life* (New York: Free Press, 2002), 158.

19. Nicholi, *Question of God*, 158.

20. Barbara Fresko and Cheruta Wertheim, "Learning by Mentoring: Prospective Teachers as Mentors to Children at Risk," *Mentoring and Tutoring*, 14, no. 2 (May 2006): 149–61.

21. C. S. Lewis, *Mere Christianity* (New York: HarperOne, 2001), 136–37.

CHAPTER 5: WHY DO I HURT?

1. Udo Middelmann, *The Innocence of God: Does God Ordain Evil?* (Colorado Springs, CO: Paternoster, 2007), 2.

2. Debarati Guha-Sapir, Philippe Hoyois, and Regina Below, "Annual Disaster Statistical Review 2012: The Numbers and Trends," Centre for Research on the Epidemiology of Disasters, August 31, 2013, http://reliefweb.int /report/world/annual-disaster-statistical-review-2012-numbers-and-trends.

3. Viktor Frankl, *Man's Search for Meaning* (Boston: Beacon, 1992), 117.

4. Norman L. Geisler, *If God, Why Evil? A New Way to Think about the Question* (Minneapolis: Bethany House, 2011), 19. Saint Augustine discusses the

problem of evil at length in *Confessions*, Book VII, which is available free online at www.ccel.org/a/augustine/confessions/confessions.html.

5. Richard Dawkins, *River out of Eden: A Darwinian View of Life* (New York: Basic Books, 1995), 133.

6. V. I. Lenin, *Collected Works*, ed. Clemens Dutt, vol. 11, *June 1906–July 1907* (Moscow: Progress, 1972), 71.

7. As Marx phrased it in the *Communist Manifesto*, the Communists' ends "can be attained only by the forcible overthrow of all existing social conditions.... The proletarians have nothing to lose but their chains. They have a world to win. Working men of all countries, unite!," *Marx/Engels Selected Works*, trans. Samuel Moore and Frederick Engels, vol. 1 (Moscow: Progress, 1969), www.marxists.org/archive/marx/works/1848/communist-manifesto/ch04.htm.

8. Lenin, *Collected Works*, ed. Andrew Rothstein, vol. 10, *November 1905–June 1906* (Moscow: Progress, 1978), 83.

9. R. J. Rummel, "How Many Did Communist Regimes Murder?," University of Hawaii, November 1993, www.hawaii.edu/powerkills/COM.ART.HTM.

10. Albert Camus, *The Myth of Sisyphus and Other Essays*, trans. Justin O'Brien (New York: Vintage, 1983), 121.

11. Al-Ghazali is quoted as saying, "The gist is that good and evil are foreordained. What is foreordained comes necessarily to be after a prior act of divine volition.... Rather, everything small and large is written and comes to be in a known and expected measure." See Eric L. Ormsby, *Theodicy in Islamic Thought: The Dispute over Al-Ghazali's "Best of All Possible Worlds"* (Princeton, NJ: Princeton University Press, 1984), 41.

12. The Quran states, "Those who believe, and whose hearts find satisfaction in the remembrance of Allah: for without doubt in the remembrance of Allah do hearts find satisfaction. For those who believe and work righteousness, is (every) blessedness, and a beautiful place of (final) return"; see *An English Interpretation of the Holy Quran*, trans. Abdullah Yusuf Ali (Bensenville, IL: Lushena Books, 2001), 13:28–29.

13. Khurshid Ahmad, introduction to *Islam: Our Choice*, comp. and ed. Ebrahim Ahmed Bawany (Jeddah, Saudi Arabia: Al-Madina, 1961), 2.

14. Marilyn Ferguson, *The Aquarian Conspiracy: Personal and Social Transformation in Our Time* (Los Angeles: Jeremy P. Tarcher, 1987), 257.

15. Shakti Gawain, another new spiritualist writer, said we experience pain because we don't trust ourselves to overcome it: "Every time you don't trust

yourself and don't follow your inner truth, you decrease your aliveness and your body will reflect this with a loss of vitality, numbness, pain, and eventually physical disease." *Living in the Light: Follow Your Inner Guidance to Create a New Life and a New World* (San Rafael, CA: New World Library, 1989), 156. Vera Alder goes even further, explaining that criminals who cause others to suffer should be celebrated because such suffering forces us to seek more urgently a connection with a higher consciousness: "A criminal or an idler will be recognized as a sick individual offering a splendid chance for wise help. Instead of being incarcerated with fellow unfortunates in the awful atmosphere of a prison, the future 'criminal' will be in much demand." Quoted in Texe Marrs, *Dark Secrets of the New Age: Satan's Plan for a One World Religion* (Wheaton, IL: Crossway, 1993), 175.

16. Jonathan Morrow, *Welcome to College: A Christ-Follower's Guide for the Journey* (Grand Rapids, MI: Kregel, 2008), 119.

17. Stephen Mitchell, trans., *Bhagavad Gita: A New Translation* (New York: Three Rivers, 2000), 47.

18. Krishna's statement represents the general tenor of Hindu writing on evil and suffering, though Hinduism is a very diverse religion and not all Hindus hold this view. Hinduism is actually a religious culture that, according to Taylor University professor of philosophy and religion Winfried Corduan, "has moved back and forth through various phases of monotheism, henotheism, polytheism and animism, with each stage retaining at least a vestigial presence in the ensuing one. There is no set of core beliefs that remains constant throughout. The name itself, actually a label devised by Westerners, simply means 'the religion of India.'" *Neighboring Faiths: A Christian Introduction to World Religions* (Downers Grove, IL: IVP Academic, 2012), 267. See also R. C. Zaehner, *Hinduism* (New York: Oxford University Press, 1983). Hinduism is primarily spread today through the practice of yoga, a meditational exercise. Whether this is harmful or not is the subject of much debate in the Christian community. For more information, see Albert Mohler's podcast "The Meaning of Yoga: A Conversation with Stephanie Syman and Doug Groothius," September 20, 2010, www.albertmohler.com/2010/09/20/the-meaning-of-yoga-a -conversation-with-stephanie-syman-and-doug-groothius/.

19. "The Four Noble Truths," A View on Buddhism, December 29, 2016, http://viewonbuddhism.org/4_noble_truths.html.

20. Walpola Sri Rahula, "The First Sermon of the Buddha," *Tricycle*, www.tricycle.com/new-buddhism/teachings-and-texts/first-sermon -buddha.

21. *Psychology Today* says emotional pain is actually worse than physical pain because it can be triggered by memories, it's hard to distract ourselves from it, it echoes through our lives, people aren't as empathetic, and it can be devastating to our self-esteem and long-term emotional health. See Guy Winch, "5 Ways Emotional Pain Is Worse Than Physical Pain: Why Emotional Pain Causes Longer Lasting Damage to Our Lives," *Psychology Today*, July 20, 2014, www.psychologytoday.com/blog/the-squeaky -wheel/201407/5-ways-emotional-pain-is-worse-physical-pain.

22. Kima Joy Taylor, quoted in "New Data Show Millions of Americans with Alcohol and Drug Addiction Could Benefit from Health Care R," Partnership for Drug-Free Kids, September 28, 2010, www.drugfree.org /new-data-show-millions-of-americans-with-alcohol-and-drug-addiction -could-benefit-from-health-care-r/.

23. "Legally Dead: Exploring the Epidemic of Prescription Drug Abuse," Rehabs.com, www.rehabs.com/explore/prescription-drug-abuse-statistics/.

24. "Youth Suicide Statistics," The Parent Resource Program, http://jasonfoundation .com/prp/facts/youth-suicide-statistics/; Dan Bilsker and Jennifer White, "The Silent Epidemic of Male Suicide," *British Columbia Medical Journal* 53, no. 10 (December 2011): 529–34, www.bcmj.org/articles/silent-epidemic-male -suicide.

25. C. S. Lewis, *Mere Christianity* (New York: HarperOne, 2001), 39.

CHAPTER 6: WE SHALL OVERCOME

1. Ernest Gordon, *To End All Wars: A True Story about the Will to Survive and the Courage to Forgive* (Grand Rapids, MI: Zondervan, 1963), 72.

2. Gordon, *To End All Wars*, 105.

3. Philip Yancey, *Where Is God When It Hurts?* (Grand Rapids, MI: Zondervan, 1990), 91.

4. See Romans 12:21; 1 John 2:13–14; 4:4; Revelation 2:7, 11, 17, 26; 3:5, 12, 21; 21:7.

5. Theologians sharpen this understanding by noting that God is omniscient— that is, possessing complete knowledge of what is possible and actual, past, present, and future. For a helpful explication of this doctrine amid challenges of Open Theism, see William Lane Craig, *What Does God Know? Reconciling Divine Foreknowledge and Human Freedom* (Norcross, GA: RZIM, 2002).

6. This summary necessarily leaves out many nuances of the free-will argument. For readers wishing to study the argument in more detail, see, in addition to the other resources from this chapter, Alvin Plantinga, *God, Freedom, and Evil* (Grand Rapids, MI: Eerdmans, 1977).

7. When it comes to explaining the fall, R. C. Sproul, a well-known Reformed theologian, said, "[God] ordained the Fall in the sense that he chose to allow it, but not in the sense that he chose to coerce it." R. C. Sproul, *Chosen by God* (Wheaton, IL: Tyndale, 1986), 97.

8. Norman Geisler offers many additional examples in support of this thesis, that "some physical evil is the byproduct of a good process." Norman L. Geisler, *If God, Why Evil? A New Way to Think about the Question* (Minneapolis: Bethany House, 2011), 75.

9. Philosopher William Lane Craig wrote an entire book about God's knowledge titled *Divine Foreknowledge and Human Freedom*. In it, Craig argues for a position called Molinism, which was first articulated by a Jesuit priest named Luis de Molina (AD 1535–1600). Molina proposed a middle knowledge view of God that avoided the idea that God directly causes every single action in the universe (divine determinism) and also its extreme opposite, open theism—that although God is knowledgeable enough to make very accurate guesses about what will or won't happen in the future, he does not know with certainty. Craig said that because God knows all things, he knows the choices free creatures make under every possible circumstance. And yet he still leaves them free to make those choices. As we make choices, God knows what will happen as a result and is working things out so that when we arrive at the place where our free choices take us, we will see that he has worked in such a way that his good, desired end is achieved. See William Lane Craig, *Divine Foreknowledge and Human Freedom: The Coherence of Theism; Omniscience* (Leiden, The Netherlands: E. J. Brill, 1991). Author's note: Recognizing God's mercy, some people have stopped taking responsibility for their actions, saying, "God will redeem me and anyone who gets hurt in the process." This is arrogant, twisted, and sick thinking. God hates it. It involves trying to play God by deciding who should experience his grace rather than extending it to everyone, as we are commanded to do.

10. C. S. Lewis, *The Problem of Pain* (New York: HarperOne, 2015).

11. Some say evil is personal as well. Though the Bible is not explicitly clear on this, there are good reasons to think that sin got "kicked off" when an arch-angel named Lucifer, or Satan, tried to overthrow God. Satan then possessed a serpent in the garden of Eden and tempted Adam and Eve to sin (see Genesis 3). In Revelation 12:9 and 20:2, this "ancient serpent" is described

as "the devil and Satan." So how could a creature such as Satan, who had no sin nature, fall into sin and cause humanity to fall in his wake? Perhaps, as Norman Geisler suggested, no one caused Lucifer to sin; he caused his own sin. Geisler wrote, "Many consider this an insoluble mystery. But is it? Not really—not once we understand what free choice entails. The best way to comprehend the basis of a free act is to examine the three possible alternatives. A free act is either uncaused, caused by another, or self-caused. That is, it is undetermined, determined by another, or self-determined. No action can be uncaused (undetermined); that would be a violation of the law of causality (every event has a cause). Neither can a free act be caused by another, for if someone or something else caused the action, it is not ours (not from our free choice) and we would not be responsible for it. Hence, all free actions must be self-caused—that is, caused by oneself. Now we can answer the question 'Who caused Lucifer to sin?' No one did. He is the cause of his own sin. Sin is a self-caused action, one for which we cannot blame anyone or anything else. Who caused the first sin? Lucifer. How did he cause it? By the power of free choice, which God gave him." Norman L. Geisler, *If God, Why Evil? A New Way to Think about the Question* (Minneapolis: Bethany House, 2011), 30–31. It should be noted that Geisler's point is highly disputed. Do angels have free will? Did they once but no longer? Scripture doesn't tell us. If angels are free, we'd expect more to have fallen since then, but we have no scriptural record of this happening. Also, if Lucifer was the cause of Adam and Eve's sin, was there an agent who caused his own sin? Because Scripture says little about these matters, we are left with the need to be humble in our thoughts about such things.

12. Edward Shillito, "Jesus of the Scars," in D. A. Carson, *The Gospel according to John*, The Pillar New Testament Commentary (Grand Rapids, MI: Eerdmans, 1991), 647.

13. John Stott, quoted in Randy Alcorn, *If God Is Good: Faith in the Midst of Suffering and Evil* (Colorado Springs, CO: Multnomah Books, 2009), 217.

14. William Lane Craig, *On Guard: Defending Your Faith with Reason and Precision* (Colorado Springs, CO: David C Cook, 2010), 173.

15. Scott C. Todd, *Fast Living: How the Church Will End Extreme Poverty* (Colorado Springs, CO: Compassion International, 2011), 37.

16. "Key Facts from JMP 2015 Report," World Health Organization, www.who.int/water_sanitation_health/monitoring/jmp-2015-key-facts/en/.

17. Carol Pearson, "Tuberculosis Cases Down, Disease Still a Major Killer," VOA, October 18, 2012, www.voanews.com/content/tb-cases-down-but-disease-still-a-major-killer/1528710.html.

18. "Poliomyelitis," World Health Organization, April 2016, www.who.int /mediacentre/factsheets/fs114/en/.

19. "World Malaria Report 2011," World Health Organization, www.who.int /malaria/world_malaria_report_2011/en/.

20. Dallas Willard, "Frank Laubach's *Letters by a Modern Mystic*," www.dwillard .org/articles/artview.asp?artID=43.

21. Karl Menninger, quoted in Therese Borchard, "Want to Lessen Your Depression? Help Someone," *Everyday Health*, March 6, 2015, www.everydayhealth.com/columns/therese-borchard-sanity-break /want-lessen-your-depression-help-someone/.

22. See www.motherteresa.org for more information on ministries, such as the Kalighat Home for the Dying, serving "the least of these" (Matt. 25:40).

23. Alcorn, *If God Is Good*, 449.

24. Yancey, *Where Is God When It Hurts?*, 232.

CHAPTER 7: DOES MY LIFE HAVE MEANING?

1. Elizabeth Nietzsche, quoted in Julian Young, *Friedrich Nietzsche: A Philosophical Biography* (New York: Cambridge University Press, 2010), 18.

2. Nietzsche, quoted in Young, *Nietzsche*, 18.

3. Nietzsche, quoted in Young, *Nietzsche*, 34.

4. Friedrich Nietzsche, *The Gay Science: With a Prelude in Rhymes and an Appendix of Songs*, trans. Walter Kaufmann (New York: Vintage Books, 1974), 181. For a clear and understandable analysis of Nietzsche's anti-God and anti-Christ positions, see chapter 9 of Will Durant, *The Story of Philosophy: The Lives and Opinions of the Great Philosophers of the Western World* (New York: Simon and Schuster, 2005).

5. The rise of Nazism, like the rise of Marxism, demonstrates the relationship between bad philosophies and bad government. In the case of the Nazis, Nietzsche's influence is undeniable. During World War I, tens of thousands of copies of Nietzsche's book *Thus Spake Zarathustra*, in which he told the parable of the madman and discussed his superman ideal, were distributed. A few years later, Adolf Hitler published *Mein Kampf*, presenting himself to be a superman. The Nazis spoke constantly of Nietzsche. "No one who lived in the Third Reich could have failed to be impressed by Nietzsche's influence on it," wrote William L. Shirer in his highly regarded history of

the Nazis. *The Rise and Fall of the Third Reich: A History of Nazi Germany* (New York: Simon and Schuster, 1990), 100.

6. Chris Turner, "Ultimate Purpose and Meaning: Some Say They Pursue It, Others Do Not," LifeWay, December 27, 2011, www.lifeway.com/Article /Research-Ultimate-purpose-and-meaning.

7. William Damon, *The Path to Purpose: How Young People Find Their Calling in Life* (New York: Free Press, 2008), 8.

8. According to Maurice R. Stein, "Humanist sociology views society as an historically evolving enterprise that can only be understood through the struggle to liberate human potentialities." "On the Limits of Professional Thought," in John F. Glass and John R. Staude, eds., *Humanistic Society: Today's Challenge to Sociology* (Pacific Palisades, CA: Goodyear, 1972), 165.

9. See "Who Are the Brights?," The Brights, www.the-brights.net.

10. Ivan Pavlov, in a statement to his assistants on February 21, 1936, according to W. Horsley Gantt, introduction to *Conditioned Reflexes and Psychiatry: Lectures on Conditioned Reflexes* (New York: International Publishers, 1963), 34.

11. *Enemy at the Gates*, directed by Jean-Jacques Annaud (Paramount Pictures, 2001).

12. Tolle doesn't like words like *I* and *my* because, he said, they trick us into thinking we have personalities and souls separate from all other souls: "In normal everyday usage, 'I' embodies the primordial error, a misperception of who you are, an illusory sense of identity. This is the ego." *A New Earth: Awakening to Your Life's Purpose* (New York: Dutton, 2005), 27.

13. The Dalai Lama, *A Profound Mind: Cultivating Wisdom in Everyday Life*, ed. Nicholas Vreeland (New York: Harmony Books, 2011), ix.

14. Ken Carey (speech, Whole Life Expo, Los Angeles, February 1987).

15. *An English Interpretation of the Holy Quran*, trans. Abdullah Yusuf Ali (Bensenville, IL: Lushena Books, 2001).

16. As the famous Arab historian Ibn Khaldun (1332–1406) said, "In the Muslim community, the holy war is a religious duty, because of the univer- salism of the (Muslim) mission and (the obligation to) convert everybody to Islam either by persuasion or by force." Quoted in Colin Chapman, *Cross and Crescent: Responding to the Challenge of Islam* (Downers Grove, IL: InterVarsity, 2003), 293.

17. Morten Storm, with Paul Cruickshank and Tim Lister, *Agent Storm: My Life inside Al Qaeda and the CIA* (New York: Grove, 2014), 238.

18. For more statistics and references, see this infographic: "Data Never Sleeps: How Much Data Is Generated Every Minute?," Visually, July 11, 2012, http://visual.ly/data-never-sleeps.

19. Michel Foucault, *The Order of Things: An Archaeology of the Human Sciences* (New York: Vintage Books, 1994), 385. Students reading Foucault need to keep in mind his own admission: "I am fully aware that I have never written anything other than fictions." Quoted in Hubert L. Dreyfus and Paul Rabinow, *Michel Foucault: Beyond Structuralism and Hermeneutics*, 2nd ed. (Chicago: University of Chicago Press, 1983), 204.

20. John Coffey, *Life after the Death of God? Michel Foucault and Postmodern Atheism* (Cambridge, UK: Cambridge Papers, 1996), 1.

21. Postmodernists who identify with the Christian tradition, of which there are a few who proceed through academic arguments rather than popular ones, also posit a "hermeneutics of finitude"—that we are finite and limited in our humanness, so we must be humble or chastened in our claims. We must be careful in saying this, though. If we take this view too far, we might end up saying we cannot understand things Scripture clearly commands us to understand, in which case we make an idol out of our reluctance. This is not humility; it is stubborn sinfulness.

22. David F. Ruccio and Jack Amariglio, *Postmodern Moments in Modern Economics* (Princeton, NJ: Princeton University Press, 2003), 167.

23. Ruccio and Amariglio, *Postmodern Moments*, 134.

24. Nazi brutality would most likely have been opposed by Nietzsche, but he would have had no basis for his opposition, other than his own will to power (which he expressed with violent flippancy when he said that anti-Semites should be shot).

25. Shirer, *The Rise and Fall of the Third Reich*, 111.

CHAPTER 8: HEARING THE CALL

1. Morten Storm, with Paul Cruickshank and Tim Lister, *Agent Storm: My Life inside Al Qaeda and the CIA* (New York: Grove, 2014), 227.

2. Abraham Kuyper, *Near unto God: Daily Meditations Adapted for Contemporary Christians by James C. Schaap* (Grand Rapids, MI: CRC, 1997), 7.

3. Clarence Darrow, quoted in James A. Haught, *2,000 Years of Disbelief: Famous People with the Courage to Doubt* (New York: Prometheus Books, 1996), 222.

4. Twenty One Pilots, "Stressed Out," *Blurryface* © 2015 Warner-Tamerlane Publishing Corp. and Stryker Joseph Music.

5. See *abad*, Strong's Hebrew reference number 5647, in Robert L. Thomas, ed., *New American Standard Exhaustive Concordance of the Bible: Hebrew-Aramaic and Greek Dictionaries* (Nashville: Holman, 1981), 1569.

6. James E. Marcia, based on the work of psychologist Erik Erikson, developed a series of categories used to examine what shapes identity. See "Identity in Adolescence" in *Handbook of Adolescent Psychology*, ed. Joseph Adelson (New York: Wiley and Sons, 1980), 159–87.

7. Elaine Scarry, *On Beauty and Being Just* (Princeton, NJ: Princeton University Press, 1999), 112.

8. Arthur F. Miller, *Designed for Life: Hardwired, Empowered, Purposed; The Birthright of Every Human Being* (Charlotte, NC: Life(n) Media, 2006), 42.

9. Howard G. Hendricks, *Color outside the Lines: Learning the Art of Creativity* (Nashville: Thomas Nelson, 1998), 76.

10. Mihály Csíkszentmihályi and Reed Larson, *Being Adolescent: Conflict and Growth in the Teenage Years* (New York: Basic Books, 1984).

11. "The Experience of Leisure in Adolescence: Abstract," Illinois Experts, https://experts.illinois.edu/en/publications/the-experience-of-leisure-in-adolescence.

12. Jeanne Nakamura and Mihály Csíkszentmihályi, "Flow Theory and Research," in *The Oxford Handbook of Positive Psychology*, ed. Shane J. Lopez and C. R. Snyder, 2nd ed. (New York: Oxford University Press, 2009), 195–96.

13. Mihály Csíkszentmihályi, *Flow and the Foundations of Positive Psychology: The Collected Works of Mihály Csíkszentmihályi* (New York: Springer, 2014), 10.

CHAPTER 9: WHY CAN'T WE JUST GET ALONG?

1. Aryn Baker, "Who Killed Abdullah Azzam?," *Time*, June 18, 2009, http://content.time.com/time/specials/packages/article/0,28804,1902809_1902810_1905173-1,00.html.

2. Though it cannot be proved, some believe that Osama bin Laden was responsible for the death of Abdullah Azzam. Azzam had many enemies, but no one benefited more than bin Laden from his death. With Azzam's death, bin Laden was able to secure his power in Afghanistan and turn the training camps of the mujahideen into facilities for training fighters

to forcefully spread Islam throughout the world; see "Profile: Abdullah Azzam," History Commons, www.historycommons.org/entity .jsp?entity=abdullah_azzam.

3. Mary Anne Weaver, "Her Majesty's Jihadists: More British Muslims Have Joined Islamist Militant Groups Than Serve in the Country's Armed Forces. How to Understand the Pull of Jihad," *New York Times*, April 14, 2015, www.nytimes.com/2015/04/19/magazine/her-majestys-jihadists .html?_r=0.

4. Chris Hedges, "What Every Person Should Know about War," *New York Times*, July 6, 2003, www.nytimes.com/2003/07/06/books/chapters/0713 -1st-hedges.html. See also Chris Hedges, *What Every Person Should Know about War* (New York: Free Press, 2003).

5. Peter Wood, *A Bee in the Mouth: Anger in America Now* (New York: Encounter Books, 2006), 2.

6. Wood, *Bee in the Mouth*, 4.

7. G. K. Chesterton, quoted in Ravi Zacharias, ed., *Beyond Opinion: Living the Faith We Defend* (Nashville: Thomas Nelson, 2007), 206.

8. John de Graaf, David Wann, and Thomas H. Naylor, *Affluenza: How Overconsumption Is Killing Us—and How We Can Fight Back*, 3rd ed. (San Francisco: Berrett-Koehler, 2014), 1.

9. Jeremy Bentham, quoted in Raymond Wacks, *Law: A Very Short Introduction* (Oxford: Oxford University Press, 2008), 23.

10. Mark Reader, "Humanism and Politics," *Humanist* 35, no. 6 (1975): 38.

11. Derek Bok, quoted in Zach Miners, "How Government Can Make the American Public Happy," *U.S. News*, April 30, 2010, www.usnews.com /opinion/articles/2010/04/30/how-government-can-make-the-american -public-happy-life-liberty-and-the-pursuit-of-happiness.

12. Mary Shelley, *Frankenstein: Or, the Modern Prometheus* (New York: Signet, 1994), 95.

13. Shelley, *Frankenstein*, 96. J. F. Baldwin's *The Deadliest Monster: A Christian Introduction to Worldviews* (New Braunfels, TX: Fishermen Press, 2001) is an excellent book exploring the view of human nature in Shelley's *Frankenstein* and Robert Louis Stevenson's *Strange Case of Dr. Jekyll and Mr. Hyde*.

14. Robert Tannenbaum and Sheldon A. Davis, "Values, Man and Organizations," in John F. Glass and John R. Staude, eds., *Humanistic*

Society: Today's Challenge to Sociology (Pacific Palisades, CA: Goodyear, 1972), 352.

15. John Rawls, *A Theory of Justice* (Cambridge, MA: Belknap, 2003), 4.

16. See Jean Baudrillard, *The Gulf War Did Not Take Place*, trans. Paul Patton (Bloomington, IN: Indiana University Press, 1995).

17. Eckhart Tolle, *A New Earth: Awakening to Your Life's Purpose* (New York: Dutton, 2005), 51.

18. Meher Baba, *The Mastery of Consciousness: An Introduction and Guide to Practical Mysticism and Methods of Spiritual Development*, comp. and ed. Allan Y. Cohen (New York: Harper and Row, 1977), 23.

19. Michael Bernard Beckwith, quoted in Rhonda Byrne, *The Secret* (New York: Atria Books, 2006), 147.

20. Tolle, *New Earth*, 191.

21. Quran 3:83, *The Qur'an: English Meanings* trans. Saheeh International (London: Al-Muntada, Al-Islami, 2004). See also Quran 8 and 9. Ahmad ibn Naqib al-Misri points out that "it is offensive to conduct a military expedition against hostile non-Muslims without the caliph's permission." But he further notes that if there is no caliph (Muslim head of a country), no permission is required. Muslims may then wage war as they see fit. Ahmad ibn Naqib al-Misri, *Reliance of the Traveller: A Classic Manual of Islamic Sacred Law*, trans. Nuh Ha Mim Keller (Beltsville, MD: Amana, 1994), 602.

22. From personal conversations with Nabeel Qureshi, May 2013.

23. "What Do We Make of Radical Islamicism?," *Summit Journal* 13, no. 1, (January 2013): 1, 3, www.summit.org/media/journal/2013-01_Summit _Journal-WEB.pdf.

24. J. D., "How Many People Convert to Islam?," *Economist*, September 30, 2013, www.economist.com/blogs/economist-explains/2013/09 /economist-explains-17.

25. Ivan Bahryany, "I Accuse," in S. O. Pidhainy, ed., *The Black Deeds of the Kremlin: A White Book* (Toronto: Basilian Press, 1953), 1:14. Robert Conquest, in *The Harvest of Sorrow: Soviet Collectivization and the Terror-Famine* (New York: Oxford University, 1986), 305, places the figure at 14.5 million.

26. See Paul Berman, "The Cult of Che: Don't Applaud the *Motorcycle Diaries*," *Slate*, September 24, 2004, www.slate.com/id/2107100/.

27. Stéphane Courtois, "Introduction: The Crimes of Communism," in Stéphane Courtois et al., *The Black Book of Communism: Crimes, Terror, Repression* (Cambridge, MA: Harvard University Press, 1999), 2.

28. Alexander N. Yakovlev, in his important 2002 work *A Century of Violence in Soviet Russia* (New Haven, CT: Yale University Press, 2002), estimated that Stalin alone killed more than sixty million.

29. The latest figures of more than seventy million killed under China's Mao Tse-tung are recorded by Jung Chang and Jon Halliday in their seminal work *Mao: The Unknown Story* (New York: Anchor Books, 2006).

30. Referenced in an earlier chapter, political scientist R. J. Rummel maintained a detailed website with spreadsheets documenting what he called democide, government-sponsored mass murder and genocide; see "How Many Did Communist Regimes Murder?," University of Hawaii, November 1993, www.hawaii.edu/powerkills/COM.ART.HTM.

CHAPTER 10: PEACE WINS

1. Tim Townsend, *Mission at Nuremberg: An American Army Chaplain and the Trial of the Nazis* (New York: William Morrow, 2014), 251.

2. Warren Cole Smith and John Stonestreet, *Restoring All Things: God's Audacious Plan to Change the World through Everyday People* (Grand Rapids, MI: Baker, 2015), 48.

3. "The 10 Most Dangerous U.S. Cities," *Forbes*, www.forbes.com/pictures /mlj45jggj/1-detroit/#754fbf7a7705.

4. Commission on Children at Risk, *Hardwired to Connect: The New Scientific Case for Authoritative Communities* (New York: Institute for American Values, 2003), 8.

5. Andy Crouch, *Culture Making: Recovering Our Creative Calling* (Downers Grove, IL: InterVarsity, 2008), 183.

6. Crouch, *Culture Making*, 105.

7. Andrew Zolli and Ann Marie Healy, *Resilience: Why Things Bounce Back* (New York: Free Press, 2012), 237.

8. William Isaacs, *Dialogue and the Art of Thinking Together: A Pioneering Approach to Communicating in Business and in Life* (New York: Currency, 1999), 165.

9. Isaacs, *Dialogue*, 19 (emphasis in the original).

10. Isaacs, *Dialogue*, 19.

11. Miller McPherson, Lynn Smith-Lovin, and Matthew E. Brashears, "Social Isolation in America: Changes in Core Discussion Networks over Two Decades," *American Sociological Review* 71, no. 3 (June 2006): 353–75.

12. Michael Price, "Alone in the Crowd: Sherry Turkle Says Social Networking Is Eroding Our Ability to Live Comfortably Offline," American Psychological Association, June 2011, www.apa.org/monitor/2011/06/social-networking.aspx.

CHAPTER 11: IS THERE ANY HOPE FOR THE WORLD?

1. "Fly with Us: Ready to Become an Astronaut?," Virgin Galactic, www.virgingalactic.com/human-spaceflight/fly-with-us/; "The Virgin Galactic Space Experience," Galactic Experiences by DePrez, www.galacticexperiencesbydeprez.com/experience.shtml.

2. "Welcome to Virgin Galactic," Virgin Galactic, http://sites.virtuoso.com/virgingalactic/virgingalactic/documents/vg_overview.pdf.

3. David Lester, "Hopelessness in Undergraduate Students around the World: A Review," *Journal of Affective Disorders* 150, no. 3 (September 2013): 1204–8.

4. Thomas Hobbes, *Leviathan: With Selected Variants from the Latin Edition of 1668*, ed. Edwin Curley (Indianapolis: Hackett, 1994), 76.

5. Sylvia Nasar, *Grand Pursuit: The Story of Economic Genius* (New York: Simon and Schuster, 2011), xiii–xiv.

6. J. B. Bury, quoted in Robert H. Nelson, "*Silent Spring* as Secular Religion," in Andrew Morriss, Roger Meiners, and Pierre Desrochers, eds., "*Silent Spring*" at 50: The False Crises of Rachel Carson* (Washington, DC: Cato Institute, 2012), 70.

7. R. J. Rummel, *Death by Government* (New Brunswick, NJ: Transaction, 1994).

8. Erich Fromm, *The Dogma of Christ: And Other Essays on Religion, Psychology, and Culture* (New York: Henry Holt, 1963), 101 (emphasis in the original).

9. This quote is taken from an address given by Dorothy L. Sayers called "The Other Six Deadly Sins," given to the Public Morality Council, Caxton Hall, Westminster, October 23, 1941. The full quote is as follows: "The sixth deadly sin is named by the Church *acedia* or *sloth*. In the world it calls itself tolerance; but in hell it is called despair. It is the accomplice of the other sins and their worst punishment. It is the sin that believes in nothing, cares for nothing, seeks to know nothing, interferes with nothing, enjoys nothing, loves nothing, hates nothing, finds purpose in nothing, lives for nothing, and remains alive only because there is nothing it would

die for. We have known it far too well for many years. The only thing perhaps that we have not known about it is that it is mortal sin." Dorothy L. Sayers, *Letters to a Diminished Church: Passionate Arguments for the Relevance of Christian Doctrine* (Nashville: Thomas Nelson, 2004), 98.

10. Green Day, "Boulevard of Broken Dreams" © 2004 WB Music Corp. and Green Daze Music.

11. "Resource Depletion," Center for Ecoliteracy, www.ecoliteracy.org/issues /resource-depletion#issue-expanded. (Information no longer posted on site as of July 23, 2016.)

12. Paul Watson, "The Beginning of the End for Life as We Know It on Planet Earth?," Sea Shepherd Conservation Society, May 4, 2007, www.seashepherd.org/commentary-and-editorials/2008/10/30/the -beginning-of-the-end-for-life-as-we-know-it-on-planet-earth-340.

13. Edwin Arthur Burtt, *Types of Religious Philosophy* (New York: Harper and Brothers, 1939), 353. Clearly, the secularist has no patience with the anthropic principle, which contends that the world was tailored for man's existence. For an excellent defense of this principle, see Roy Abraham Varghese, ed., *The Intellectuals Speak Out about God: A Handbook for the Christian Student in a Secular Society* (Dallas: Lewis and Stanley, 1984), 102ff.

14. Marvin Minsky, quoted in Brad Darrach, "Meet Shaky, the First Electronic Person: The Fascinating and Fearsome Reality of a Machine with a Mind of Its Own," *Life*, November 20, 1970, 68.

15. Jacques Berlinerblau, *How to Be Secular: A Call to Arms for Religious Freedom* (New York: Houghton Mifflin Harcourt, 2012), 180.

16. Julian Huxley, *Essays of a Humanist* (London: Chatto and Windus, 1964), 77.

17. Nick Bostrom, "A History of Transhumanist Thought," *Journal of Evolution and Technology* 14, no. 1 (April 2005): 1–25, https://pdfs.semanticscholar .org/0937/735acdf4d904c6b637c29c41876ed13024a3.pdf.

18. Paul Kurtz and Edwin H. Wilson, "Humanist Manifesto II," *Humanist 33*, no. 5 (1973): 6.

19. Chris Brockman, *What about Gods?* (Amherst, NY: Prometheus Books, 1978).

20. Karl Marx and Frederick Engels, *Collected Works*, vol. 6, *1845–48* (London: Lawrence and Wishart, 1976), 487.

21. Karl Marx, *A Contribution to the Critique of Political Economy*, trans. N. I. Stone (Chicago: Charles H. Kerr, 1911); on page 12, Marx said, "With the

change of the economic foundation the entire immense superstructure is more or less rapidly transformed."

22. Marx and Engels, *Collected Works*, vol. 5, *1845–47*, 8.

23. "Remembered Rapture: The Writer at Work," Macmillan, http://us.macmillan .com/rememberedrapture/bellhooks. The name *bell hooks* is the name of hook's great-grandmother, adopted as a pen name, and placed in lowercase, according to her *Wikipedia* entry, because it "signifies what is most important in her works: the 'substance of books, not who I am.'" See "bell hooks," *Wikipedia*, last modified February 25, 2017, http://en.wikipedia.org/wiki /Bell_hooks.

24. bell hooks, quoted in David Horowitz, *The Professors: The 101 Most Dangerous Academics in America* (Washington, DC: Regnery, 2006), 225.

25. Postmodernists were not the first to offer such a view of knowledge. Bertrand Russell held a similar view, that "all truths are particular truths." Mary Midgley, *Evolution as a Religion: Strange Hopes and Stranger Fears* (London: Routledge Classics, 2002), 127. Midgley offers a classic critique of this position, referencing Ludwig Wittgenstein's thought: "Particular propositions cannot always be prior to general ones. Both are elements in language, which is itself an element in our whole system of behaviour. In a crucial sense, the whole is always prior to its parts. And unquestionably this kind of belief in a law-abiding universe … is a precondition of any possible physical science."

26. David F. Ruccio and Jack Amariglio, *Postmodern Moments in Modern Economics* (Princeton, NJ: Princeton University Press, 2003), 134. Christian postmoderns such as James K. A. Smith, Merold Westphal, Nancey Murphy, Stanley Hauerwas, and Alasdair MacIntyre would disagree strongly with this claim, but I would press them to identify a philosophical or theological basis for such a nature that transcends culture or interpretation.

27. Deepak Chopra and Leonard Mlodinow, *War of the Worldviews: Where Science and Spirituality Meet—and Do Not* (New York: Three Rivers, 2012), 304.

28. George Lucas seemed conscious of how his movies served as teaching tools: "I've always tried to be aware of what I say in my films, because all of us who make motion pictures are teachers," Lucas said. "Teachers with very loud voices." Quoted in "George Lucas: Heroes, Myths and Magic; About George Lucas," PBS, January 13, 2004, www.pbs.org/wnet/americanmasters /database/lucas_g.html.

29. Eckhart Tolle, *A New Earth: Awakening to Your Life's Purpose* (New York: Dutton, 2005), 5.

30. John L. Esposito is a respected professor of Islamic studies at Georgetown University, and Dalia Mogahed is one of the most influential Muslim women in the world. "What Makes a Muslim Radical?," *Foreign Policy*, November 16, 2006, http://media.gallup.com/WorldPoll/PDF /MWSRRadical022207.pdf.

31. Urbain Vermeulen, quoted in Geert Wilders, *Marked for Death: Islam's War against the West and Me* (Washington, DC: Regnery, 2012), 69.

32. Badru D. Kateregga said, "The Christian witness, that man is created in the 'image and likeness of God,' is not the same as the Muslim witness. Although God breathed into man his spirit, as both Christians and Muslims believe, for Islam the only divine qualities entrusted to humans as a result of God's breath were those of knowledge, will, and power of action. If people use these divine qualities rightly in understanding God and following his law strictly, then he has nothing to fear in the present or the future, and no sorrow for the past." Badru D. Kateregga and David W. Shenk, *Islam and Christianity: A Muslim and a Christian in Dialogue*, in *The World of Islam: Resources for Understanding 2.0* (Colorado Springs, CO: Global Mapping International, 2006), CD-ROM, 5350.

33. Islamic scholar Khurshid Ahmad said, "Jihad has been made obligatory, which means that the individual should, when the occasion arises, offer even his life for the defense and protection of Islam and the Islamic state." Khurshid Ahmad, ed., *Islam: Its Meaning and Message*, 3rd ed. (Leicester, UK: Islamic Foundation, 1999), 39.

34. Colin Chapman quotes Zaki Badawi about the inability of Islam to develop a theology or political system that doesn't involve being in control: "As we know, the history of Islam as a faith is also the history of a state and a community of believers living by Divine law. The Muslims, jurists and theologians, have always expounded Islam as both a Government and a faith. This reflects the historical fact that Muslims, from the start, lived under their own law. Muslim theologians naturally produced a theology with this in view—it is a theology of the majority. Being a minority was not seriously considered or even contemplated. The theologians were divided in their attitude to the question of minority status. Some declared that it should not take place; that is to say that a Muslim is forbidden to live for any lengthy period under non-Muslim rule. Others suggested that a Muslim living under non-Muslim rule is under no obligation to follow the law of Islam in matters of public law. Neither of these two extremes is satisfactory. Throughout the history of Islam some pockets of Muslims lived under the sway of non-Muslim rulers, often without an alternative. They nonetheless felt sufficiently committed to their faith to attempt

to regulate their lives in accordance with its rules and regulations in so far as their circumstances permitted. In other words, the practice of the community rather than the theories of the theologians provided a solution. Nevertheless Muslim theology offers, up to the present, no systematic formulation of the status of being a minority. The question is being examined. It is hoped that the matter will be brought to focus and that Muslim theologians from all over the Muslim world will delve into this thorny subject to allay the conscience of the many Muslims living in the West and also to chart a course for Islamic survival, even revival, in a secular society." Colin Chapman, *Cross and Crescent: Responding to the Challenge of Islam* (Downers Grove, IL: InterVarsity, 2003), 149–50.

35. Paul Marshall, Lela Gilbert, and Nina Shea, *Persecuted: The Global Assault on Christians* (Nashville: Thomas Nelson, 2013), 123.

36. Will Durant, *The Story of Civilization*, vol. 6, *The Reformation* (New York: Simon and Schuster, 1957), 190.

CHAPTER 12: HOPE ENDURES

1. Mindy Belz, *They Say We Are Infidels: On the Run from ISIS with Persecuted Christians in the Middle East* (Carol Stream, IL: Tyndale, 2016).

2. J. R. R. Tolkien, *The Fellowship of the Ring* (New York: Houghton Mifflin Harcourt, 2014), 339.

3. Hesiod, Bruce MacLennan, trans., "Pandora: Hesiod, *Works and Days*, 53–105," 1995, www.stoa.org/diotima/anthology/hes_pandora.shtml.

4. Nassim Nicholas Taleb, *Antifragile: Things That Gain from Disorder* (New York: Random House, 2012), 107.

5. Andrew Zolli and Ann Marie Healy, *Resilience: Why Things Bounce Back* (New York: Free Press, 2012), 7.

6. F. W. Robertson, *F. W. Robertson's Sermons on Religion and Life* (Whitefish, MT: Kessinger, 2006), 79.

7. Jürgen Habermas, *Time of Transitions*, trans. Ciaran Cronin and Max Pensky (Cambridge, UK: Polity, 2006), 150–51 (translation of an interview from 1999).

8. Luc Ferry, *A Brief History of Thought: A Philosophical Guide to Living*, trans. Theo Cuffe (New York: Harper Perennial, 2011), 72.

9. Daniel James Devine, "Michigan's Homeless Makeover," *World*, August 8, 2015, 54–56.

10. Kristen Jordan Shamus, "Salvation, Healing for Addicts in the Valley of Death," *Detroit Free Press*, July 24, 2016, www.freep.com/story/life/family/kristen -jordan-shamus/2016/07/23/salvation-healing-addicts-valley-death/86721446/.

11. Belz, *They Say We Are Infidels*, 296.

12. Belz, *They Say We Are Infidels*, 291.

13. Timothy Keller, *Prayer: Experiencing Awe and Intimacy with God* (New York: Dutton, 2014), 229.

14. Mindy Belz, "Staying the Course: Bishop Antoine Audo and the Long-Suffering, War-Torn, Not-Going-Anywhere Christians of Syria," *World*, December 14, 2013, https://world.wng.org/2013/11/staying_the_course.

15. Personal and email conversations with Mindy Belz, August 2016.

16. Tolkien, *Fellowship of the Ring*, 339.

CHAPTER 13: IS GOD EVEN RELEVANT?

1. Craig M. Gay, *The Way of the (Modern) World: Or, Why It's Tempting to Live as If God Doesn't Exist* (Grand Rapids, MI: Eerdmans, 1998), 239.

2. C. S. Lewis, *The Weight of Glory: And Other Addresses* (New York: HarperOne, 2001), 140.

3. A. W. Tozer, *The Knowledge of the Holy: The Attributes of God; Their Meaning in the Christian Life* (New York: HarperOne, 1961), 1.

4. For more information, see Francis S. Collins, *The Language of God: A Scientist Presents Evidence for Belief* (New York: Free Press, 2007).

5. These three books are *Understanding the Faith: A Survey of Christian Apologetics* (Colorado Springs, CO: David C Cook, 2016); *Understanding the Times: A Survey of Competing Worldviews* (Colorado Springs, CO: David C Cook, 2015); and *Understanding the Culture: A Survey of Social Engagement* (Colorado Springs, CO: David C Cook, 2017).

6. Carl Sagan, *Cosmos* (New York: Ballantine Books, 1980), 1.

7. Ernest Nagel, *Logic without Metaphysics: And Other Essays in the Philosophy of Science* (Glencoe, IL: Free Press, 1956), 17.

8. Nancy Pearcey said the sacred/secular divide is "the greatest barrier to liberating the power of the gospel across the whole of culture today." *Total Truth: Liberating Christianity from Its Cultural Captivity* (Wheaton, IL: Crossway, 2005), 20.

DEFEND YOUR FAITH FROM THE DANGEROUS IDEAS OF OTHER WORLDVIEWS

Only 3 percent of Americans currently have a biblical worldview. Are you and your church members among them?

This curriculum kit draws readers into the book *The Secret Battle of Ideas about God* through a seven-session DVD—with Bible teachers including Del Tackett, John Stonestreet, and Sean McDowell—and an accompanying participant's guide. The complete kit is ideal for small-group discussion, Sunday school classes, and churches.

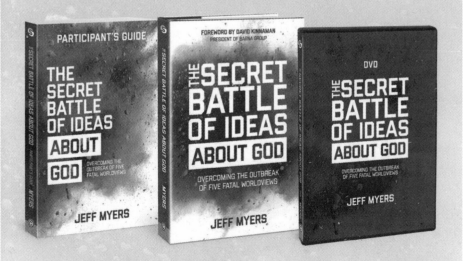

Get a special deal for your church by calling 800.323.7543

DAVID C COOK

transforming lives together

At David C Cook, we equip the local church around
the corner and around the globe to make disciples.
Come see how we are working together—go to
www.davidccook.com. Thank you!

transforming lives together